Share the Bounty

Finding God's Grace through the Spirit of Hospitality

Trust in the LORD, and do good;
Dwell in the land, and feed on His faithfulness.

[Psalm 37:3]

And when they had heard,

many wanted to praise the teaching of Christ,
and wanted to write a bright shining book with their own hands.
[*The Heliand*, ninth century, Saxon Germany]

© 2012 by Benita Long

Published in Nashville, Tennessee, by Thomas Nelson. Thomas Nelson is a registered trademark of Thomas Nelson, Inc.

Thomas Nelson, Inc., titles may be purchased in bulk for educational, business, fund-raising, or sales promotional use. For information, please e-mail SpecialMarkets@ThomasNelson.com.

Unless otherwise noted, Scripture quotations are taken from THE NEW KING JAMES VERSION. © 1982 by Thomas Nelson, Inc. Used by permission. All rights reserved.

Scriptures marked NIV are from HOLY BIBLE: NEW INTERNATIONAL VERSION®, © 1973, 1978, 1984 by International Bible Society. Used by permission of Zondervan Publishing House. All rights reserved.

Scripture quotations marked ESV are from THE ENGLISH STANDARD VERSION. © 2001 by Crossway Bibles, a division of Good New Publishers.

Library of Congress Control Number: 2012938626

ISBN: 978-1-4016-0453-0

Printed in China

12 13 14 15 16 RRD 6 5 4 3 2 1

Share the Bounty

Finding God's Grace through the Spirit of Hospitality

Benita Long

Artistic & Floral Design by Susan Wilson

Recipes & Food Styling by Ann Mitchell

Photography by Sammy Anderson

Benediction by Steve Wingfield

THOMAS NELSON
Since 1798

NASHVILLE   DALLAS   MEXICO CITY   RIO DE JANEIRO

A More Excellent Way | TABLE OF CONTENTS

Greet those who love us in the faith
[Titus 3:15]

THE CALL

Our table is set! It is spread with God's gracious plenty, the brotherly love of Jesus Christ and the warm hospitality of the Holy Spirit. And you, dear reading friend, are invited to actively participate in the feast that follows. "An Excellent Way," based on 1 Corinthians 12:36, has been prepared to assist you. It will illuminate the numerous occasions we all have to use the gift of hospitality as a means of receiving and serving others. As you peruse these pages, prepare yourself to be pleasantly surprised by a new angle of vision. Hospitality will be presented as encouragement, comfort, welcome, and accommodation. It will be reflected in celebrations of family and friendship. It will be shown to offer opportunity to pass on traditions and in alternative fashion to forge new frontiers of cultural acceptance. It will call for prayer.

Practice hospitality . . . not only to those who are joined to us by friendship or kinship but to all people with whom we are joined by nature, to the end that we might imitate our Creator. . . . Not only are spiritual provisions and heavenly gifts received through the bounty of God, but even earthly and bodily resources issue from his largess. He will have every right to ask for an accounting of these things since he gave them more by way of trusting them to be spent rather than handing them over to be kept.
[Leo 1, 400–460]

It is our desire that in every hospitable gesture you will find some measure of *hospes renit, Christus venit*, "when the guest comes, Christ comes". This radiant symbiosis of meaning and metaphor can be found in every corner of both the Old and the New Testaments. The patriarch Abraham, whose life was the unwritten law, sat at his door waiting for visitors and ran to greet them. He offered them the finest of his provisions [Genesis 18:1–8]. The widow of Zarephath's receiving Elijah [1 Kings 17:8–16] and the Shunammite's response to Elisha [2 Kings 4:9] provide but a few examples of the precedent that Jesus would continue and His followers would emulate.

We likewise have ample opportunity to entertain "angels" [Hebrews 13:2] and are fortunate in having two of Christianity's most powerful disciples to stand as witnesses. Above, the first Roman pontiff to be designated as "the Great" offers eloquent exhortation, and below, in characteristically robust style, the leader of the Protestant Reformation concurs.

We should say, Oh Lord Jesus, come to me; enjoy my bread, my wine, my silver and gold. How well it has been invested by me when I invest it in You . . . .Those who are hospitable are not receiving a human being but are receiving the Son of God Himself.
[Martin Luther, 1483–1546]

With covenant promise, in the new humanity of Christ we will be brought into the *oikos*, the household of God. Is this not a moving incentive for human extension of the same? San Benedetto da Norcia, St Benedict [480–547], instructed monastic residents to say, "Thanks be to God," each time they opened the door to a guest. What greater honor can there be?

Your sandals on your feet, and your staff in your hand

[Exodus 12:11]

PREPARE TO SHARE

The message of readiness reflected in our title verse is as valid for God's people today as it was for the ancient Israelites to whom it was first issued. After girding themselves and eating a hastily prepared meal, they were ready to participate in God's promised deliverance from Egypt. The scenario is repeated centuries later by Christ and the disciples whom Jesus instructed to take up their staffs, put on their sandals, and go forth with the new message of deliverance found in God's gospel promise. In nuance unequaled outside of Scripture, the same chapter of Mark gives us a further glimpse of Christ *who was so moved with compassion* that he willed and facilitated the feeding of thousands, saying, "You give them something to eat" [Mark 6:37]. Biblical narrative abounds with such examples of God's meeting spiritual and physical needs simultaneously. Caring and comfort are often appropriately accompanied by real sustenance for actual people. Recall Job's story.

Then all his brothers, all his sisters, and all those who had been his acquaintances before, came to him and ate food with him in his house; and they consoled him and they comforted him.
[Job 42:11]

Such faithful attention is an assurance of constancy and continuity in times of change and reorientation in the lives of others. Comfort is not something we give . . . it is something we are. It is a condition of "being with," of strengthening, of standing strong, of *forte*. Its timeliness is not determined by man but by God, which is why we aspire always to "be ready in season and out of season" [2 Timothy 4:2]. We hope that the images on the next pages will reinforce this idea for you.

The Greek word for compassion translates to mean "another life within" and is related to the word for "womb." What a beautiful blessing it is to accept the joys and challenges of others as our very own. The combined voices of a poet and an apostle are here to edify you with stout and sturdy resolve as you prepare to "Rejoice with those who rejoice, and weep with those who weep" [Romans 12:15].

Wings for the angels, but feet for men!
We may borrow the wings to find the way.
We may hope, and resolve, and aspire, and pray;
But our feet must rise, or we fall again.
[Josiah Gilbert Holland, 1819–1881]

How beautiful are the feet
of those who preach the gospel of peace,
Who bring glad tidings of good things.
[Romans 10:15]

PREPARE TO SHARE

Strawberry Rhubarb Bread

Shrimp and Yellow Rice Salad

Green Bean and Avocado Salad

Fireside Soup

Green Apple Chicken Salad

Easy Brunswick Stew

Baked Fusilli Casserole

Pork Tenderloin with Balsamic Vinegar Marinade

Asparagus Leek Quiche

Baked Lamb Stew

Peas with Prosciutto

"Let your light so shine before men,
that they may see your good works
and glorify your Father in heaven."
[Matthew 5:16]

Strawberry Rhubarb Bread

Makes 2 loaves

Bread

3 cups all-purpose flour
2 cups sugar
1 teaspoon baking soda
1 teaspoon salt
1 tablespoon cinnamon
4 eggs, beaten
1 1/4 cups vegetable oil
1 1/4 cups frozen sliced strawberries
1 1/4 cups frozen chopped rhubarb
1 cup chopped pecans

Glaze

1 1/4 cups powdered sugar
3 tablespoons milk
1/2 teaspoon vanilla extract

Preheat the oven to 350 degrees.

For the bread: Grease and flour two 9 x 5-inch loaf pans. In a large mixing bowl, combine the flour, sugar, baking soda, salt, and cinnamon. In a medium mixing bowl, combine the eggs, vegetable oil, strawberries, rhubarb, and pecans. Add the wet mixture to the dry ingredients and stir gently until blended. Divide the batter evenly between the loaf pans. Bake for 45 to 55 minutes or until a toothpick inserted into the center comes out clean. Cool the loaves in the pans for 10 minutes. Remove from the pans and cool completely on wire racks.

For the glaze: Sift the powdered sugar into a small bowl. Whisk in the milk and vanilla extract until smooth. Drizzle the glaze over the cooled bread.

If you have leftovers, wrap them tightly in plastic wrap and refrigerate for up to three days or freeze for up to a month.

But as for you, brethen,
do not grow weary in doing good.
[2 Thessalonians 3:13]

SHRIMP AND YELLOW RICE SALAD

Serves 6 to 8

Vinaigrette

3/4 teaspoon Dijon mustard

1/2 teaspoon pepper

1/2 teaspoon paprika

1/2 teaspoon sugar

2 ounces apple cider vinegar

6 ounces canola or corn oil

Salad

1 (10-ounce) package yellow rice

1 cup canned quartered artichoke hearts

1 cup halved grape tomatoes

1/4 cup sliced pimento-stuffed olives

1/4 cup chopped red bell pepper

1/4 cup chopped green onions

1/4 cup sliced celery

1/2 cup frozen green peas, thawed

1 1/2 pounds shrimp, peeled, cooked, and cut in pieces if large

For the vinaigrette: Combine the mustard, pepper, paprika, sugar, and vinegar in a small bowl. Whisk in the oil to blend. Set aside.

For the salad: Cook the rice according to package directions for firm rice. Moisten with about 1/4 cup vinaigrette. Place the rice in a large salad bowl in the refrigerator to cool.

In a large mixing bowl, combine the artichoke hearts, tomatoes, olives, red pepper, onions, celery, peas, and shrimp and stir into the cooled rice. Pour 1/2 cup of the vinaigrette over the salad and gently mix.

Reserve the remaining vinaigrette in the refrigerator until ready to serve. Remoisten with the reserved dressing just before serving and place the salad in a large salad bowl.

No act of kindness,
however small, is ever wasted.
[Aesop, 620–564 BC]

GREEN BEAN AND AVOCADO SALAD

Serves 6 to 8

Vinaigrette
2 to 4 tablespoons sugar
1/2 cup apple cider vinegar
1/2 cup canola oil

Salad
1 pound tender young green beans
1 cup sliced cherry tomatoes
1 (15-ounce) can red kidney beans, rinsed and drained
1/4 cup sliced Kalamata olives
1 medium red onion, thinly sliced into rings
1 Hass avocado, for garnish
juice of 1 lemon

For the vinaigrette: In a small bowl combine the sugar and vinegar until the sugar is dissolved. Whisk in the oil. Set aside.

For the salad: Fill a small saucepan with water and bring to a boil over high heat. Add the beans and cook until tender crisp. Plunge into a bowl of ice water to stop the cooking and hold the color. Drain. Slice into bite-size pieces.

In a salad bowl combine the green beans, tomatoes, kidney beans, olives, and onion. Pour the vinaigrette over the salad and chill for several hours.

Right before serving, slice the avocado into cubes and dip in the lemon juice to preserve the color. Top the salad with the avocado cubes and serve immediately.

Note: This is a healthy update of an old favorite from the 1970s.

If you want to lift yourself up,
lift up someone else.
[Booker Taliaferro Washington, 1856–1915]

I don't know what your destiny will be,
but one thing I do know: The only ones among you who
will be really happy are those who have sought and found how to serve.
[Albert Schweitzer, 1875–1965]

FIRESIDE SOUP

Perfect for a cold winter evening! Serve with crusty bread.

Makes 15 (one-cup) servings

1 pound hot Italian sausage
2 tablespoons vegetable oil
1 cup chopped mild onion
1 green pepper, chopped
2 cloves garlic, minced
1 pound russet potatoes, peeled and chopped
4 cups chopped cooked chicken
1 (15-ounce) can red kidney beans
1 (15-ounce) can black beans
1 (14-ounce) can chopped tomatoes
1 bay leaf
1 teaspoon chopped fresh thyme leaves (1/3 teaspoon dried)
1 teaspoon chopped fresh rosemary leaves (1/3 teaspoon dried)
6 cups chicken broth
1/2 cup red wine, optional
salt and pepper to taste

Remove the sausage from the casing and chop it into small pieces. Sauté the meat in the oil in a 4-quart stock pot. Remove the meat from the pan and sauté the onion, green pepper, and garlic until tender. Return the sausage to the pot and add the potatoes, chicken, beans, tomatoes, bay leaf, thyme, and rosemary. Add the chicken broth and wine and simmer about 4 hours.

Salt and pepper to taste. If the soup is too thin, leave the top off the pot the last few minutes to thicken. Take out the bay leaf before serving.

Joy is the holy fire that keeps our purpose warm.
[Helen Keller, 1880–1968]

GREEN APPLE CHICKEN SALAD

Serves 8 to 10

Dressing

3/4 cup good quality mayonnaise

1 tablespoon lemon juice

2 tablespoons curry powder

2 tablespoons fruit chutney, chopped

Salad

4 cups chopped cooked chicken

2 crisp green apples (such as Granny Smith) cut in small pieces, not peeled

1 cup chopped celery

4 chopped scallions, white and green parts

1/3 cup dried cranberries

1 cup chopped walnuts, toasted

For the dressing: In a small bowl combine the mayonnaise, lemon juice, curry powder, and chutney. Set aside.

For the salad: In a salad bowl combine the chicken, apples, celery, scallions, and cranberries. Pour the dressing over the salad and mix well. Chill for several hours. Top with the walnuts just before serving.

Note: This is even better the next day.

I expect to pass through this world but once.
Therefore if there is any kindness I can show or any good thing I can do for any fellow human being, let me do it now; let me not defer or neglect it, for I will not pass this way again.

All that is harmony for thee, O Universe, is in harmony with me as well. Nothing that comes at the right time for thee is too early or too late for me. Everything is fruit to me that thy seasons bring, O Nature. All things come of thee, have their being in thee, and return to thee.
[Marcus Aurelius, last of the Good Emperors, AD 121–180]

Go your way, eat the fat, drink the sweet,
and send portions to those for whom nothing is prepared.
[Nehemiah 8:10]

Easy Brunswick Stew

Serves 20

4 large bone-in chicken breasts (about 4 pounds)

2 pounds pulled pork barbecue meat

1 1/2 cups chopped white onion sautéed in 2 tablespoons butter

3 (28-ounce) cans crushed tomatoes in puree

6 ears of fresh corn, cut from cob (about 3 cups frozen or canned)

2 (10-ounce) packages frozen butter peas or butter beans, partially cooked

1 cup chili sauce (Heinz preferred)

1/2 cup Worcestershire sauce

1 to 2 tablespoons Tabasco sauce

salt and pepper to taste

In a large pot place the chicken breasts and cover with 6 cups of water. Bring to a simmer and cook until the meat is very tender. Remove the breasts from the pan, debone, and chop the chicken into small pieces. Pour the broth into a 1 1/2- to 2-gallon stock pot and add the chicken, pork, onions, tomatoes, corn, peas, chili sauce, Worcestershire sauce, and Tabasco sauce. Simmer about 45 minutes until thickened. Season with salt and pepper to taste.

Note: This stew is better when it's made a day ahead to allow the flavors to blend. It also freezes beautifully.

What do we live for if it is not
to make life less difficult for each other?
[George Eliot, 1819–1880]

Spring passes and one remembers innocence
Summer passes and one remembers exuberance
Autumn passes and one remembers reverence
Winter passes and one remembers perseverance.
[Yoko Ono, 1933–]

BAKED FUSILLI CASSEROLE

Serves 10 to 12

Meat Sauce

1 pound ground beef

1 cup chopped white onion

8 ounces sliced mushrooms

2 tablespoons olive oil

1 clove garlic, minced

1 (15-ounce) can chopped tomatoes

1 (6-ounce) can tomato paste

3/4 cup water

2 bay leaves

1 tablespoon minced fresh thyme (1 teaspoon dried)

1 tablespoon minced fresh oregano (1 teaspoon dried)

salt and pepper to taste

Pasta Layer

4 cups dry fusilli pasta (about a pound), cooked and drained

15 ounces ricotta cheese

1/3 cup chopped fresh parsley

1/2 cup grated Parmesan cheese

Cheese Topping

2 cups shredded mixed Italian cheeses or a mixture of shredded mozzarella,
    provolone, Asiago, and Parmesan cheeses

Preheat the oven to 350 degrees.

For the meat sauce: In a large skillet brown the beef, onions, and mushrooms in the olive oil until the meat is no longer pink. Add the garlic, tomatoes, tomato paste, water, bay leaves, thyme, oregano, salt, and pepper. Turn the heat to low and cook covered for about 30 minutes. Stir frequently. Check for seasonings and remove the bay leaves.

For the pasta layer: In a small bowl combine the cooked fusilli, ricotta cheese, parsley, and Parmesan cheese.

To assemble: In a 3-quart casserole place a thin layer of the meat sauce. Cover with the fusilli mixture and top with the remaining meat sauce. Sprinkle with the two cups of cheese. Bake for about 45 minutes until hot and bubbly.

We make a living by what we get,
but we make a life by what we give.
[Winston Churchill, 1874–1965]

Pork Tenderloin with Balsamic Vinegar Marinade

Serves 4 to 6

1/4 cup red balsamic vinegar
1 tablespoon honey
1 teaspoon Dijon mustard
1 tablespoon extra virgin olive oil
1 teaspoon minced fresh rosemary
cracked pepper to taste
2 (1 pound) pork tenderloins

In a small bowl whisk together the balsamic vinegar, honey, and mustard. Stir in the olive oil, rosemary, and pepper. Place the pork in a gallon-size plastic bag and pour the marinade in the bag. Seal tightly and marinate several hours or overnight in the refrigerator.

Preheat a grill to medium heat. Remove the pork from the bag. Pour the marinade into a small saucepan and warm over medium heat.

Grill the tenderloins about 20 minutes or until desired doneness, basting frequently with the marinade. Let rest about 10 minutes before slicing.

Christ has no body now on earth but yours,
no hands but yours, no feet but yours,
your eyes are the eyes through which Christ's compassion
is to look out to the earth,
yours are the feet by which He is to go about doing good
and yours are the hands by which He is to bless us now.
[St. Teresa of Avila, 1515–1582]

Now therefore, let your hands
be strengthened, and be valiant.
[2 Samuel 2:7]

Asparagus Leek Quiche

Serves 6 to 8

1 (9-inch) frozen deep-dish pie shell, unbaked

6 slices bacon

1 large leek, sliced

1 pound asparagus, rough ends removed

2 cups grated aged Swiss cheese

3 large eggs, beaten

1 1/2 cups half-and-half

salt and white pepper to taste

Preheat the oven to 425 degrees.

Fill a large pot with water, cover, and bring to a boil over high heat.

Fill the pie shell with pie weights or dried beans and bake about 7 minutes. Remove the weights and bake another 4 to 5 minutes until light brown. Remove the pie shell from the oven and set aside. Reduce the oven temperature to 325 degrees.

In a large skillet cook the bacon until crisp. Remove the bacon from the pan, crumble, and set aside. Cook the leek in the pan drippings until tender.

Cook the asparagus in simmering water until tender crisp. Immediately plunge into a bowl of ice water to hold the color and stop the cooking. Drain and cut into 1-inch pieces.

Place half of the bacon in the pie crust. Top with the leeks, asparagus, and cheese. Sprinkle the remaining bacon on top.

In a small bowl mix the eggs, half-and-half, salt, and pepper and pour over the pie. Bake 40 to 45 minutes until a knife inserted in the center comes out clean. Let cool a few minutes before serving.

Blessed be the God and Father
of our Lord Jesus Christ, the Father of mercies and God of all comfort, who comforts us in all
tribulation, that we may be able to comfort those who are in any trouble,
with the comfort with which we ourselves are comforted by God.
[2 Corinthians 1:3–4]

BAKED LAMB STEW

Serves 6 to 8

Stew

1 pound lamb, cubed

salt and pepper, divided

all-purpose flour for dusting

2 tablespoons olive oil

1 (6-ounce) package baby carrots

1 stalk celery, sliced

l large red onion, chopped

2 cloves garlic, minced

1/4 cup chopped parsley

1 teaspoon thyme

1 bay leaf

1 (14.5-ounce) can chopped tomatoes

1 (14.5-ounce) can beef broth

Potato topping

8 to 10 new potatoes, about 2 pounds

2 tablespoons butter

1/4 cup milk

1/4 cup grated Parmesan cheese

For the stew: Sprinkle the lamb cubes with salt and pepper and shake in a paper bag with a little flour to coat. Heat the oil in a Dutch oven and cook the lamb, turning to brown all the sides. Remove the meat with a slotted spoon and pour off the fat. Return the meat to the pan and add the carrots, celery, onion, garlic, parsley, thyme, bay leaf, tomatoes, and beef broth. Cover and simmer about 2 1/2 hours until the meat is very tender. Remove the top and continue to simmer until the stew is thickened. Remove the bay leaf. Taste for seasonings.

For the potato topping: Place the potatoes in a 2-quart pot, cover with water, and simmer until tender. Remove from the pot and place the potatoes in a medium mixing bowl. Add the butter and milk and mash the potatoes, skin on, until creamy. Season with salt and pepper.

To assemble: Preheat the oven to 350 degrees. Place the stew in a 1 1/2-quart round casserole and cover with the mashed potatoes. Sprinkle with the cheese.

Bake uncovered for 30 to 40 minutes, until hot and bubbly.

PEAS WITH PROSCIUTTO

Serves 6 to 8

1 cup chicken broth
2 (10- to 12-ounce) packages frozen green peas
3 tablespoons butter
2 medium shallots, thinly sliced
1/4 pound prosciutto, diced
salt and pepper

Bring the broth to a boil in a medium saucepan. Add the peas and cook 5 to 10 minutes, depending on the size. Drain the peas. In a medium skillet heat the butter and sauté the shallots until limp. Add the prosciutto and peas and sauté a few minutes until heated well. Season with salt and pepper.

There is no need to visit with words, but with benefits.
What is needed is meat and drink. If all else fails money is even acceptable, provided all is done in the name of the Creator and Author of the world.
[*Instructions,* Commodianus, third century]

Let us not love in word or in tongue, but in deed and in truth.
[1 John 3:18]

"I have called you friends"
[John 15:15]

THREE DELIGHTFUL LUNCHEONS

We opened with a chapter on meeting the needs of others, but this section was created just for you, good *freond*. Yes, you read the word correctly. Now please say it out loud. Does it sound remarkably like "friend"? Perhaps that is because freond is the early English form of the modern derivative. Even more remarkable is its original meaning, "love." By dusting off our rusty algebra, we can accept the premise that if a friend is love and God is love, it can be affirmed that God, love, and friendship are inextricably intertwined. There's just no way out of the equation! When we express love for our earthly friends in a proactive manner, we demonstrate the greater love we have for our Father and His Son. In John 15, Jesus clearly calls us friends and does so immediately after calling upon us to care for one another.

This chapter will enable you to use your hospitable talents as a means of enjoying those who have meaning in your life. One of the world's greatest lyric poets, Hafiz [1325–1389] used the expression, "The person I love lives inside of you." We have unleashed beauty and boldness so that you might exuberantly share this sentiment with those for whom you have special affection. Perhaps how well we relate to our friends here on earth says something about how prepared we are to meet our Friend for eternity.

In his 1898 widely translated book *Friendship*, Hugh Black maintains that throughout human history friendship has served as a "training ground" for divine love. Leaning heavily on Ralph Waldo Emerson, he makes a credible case that "we must be our own before we can be another's." To be a sincere friend of someone else, we must first realize who God continuously creates us to be. Use this idea to be like the woman in Luke 15: call in your friends and allow them to see you in your very best light. Allow proper space for your creative spirit to shine!

We hope that everyone who spends time among these pages will find something especially appealing. Therefore, without apology we borrow a phrase from the noted man of letters, Dr. Samuel Johnson [1709–1784] to unabashedly devote these particular pages to "the endearing elegance of female friendship."

She is a friend of mind. She gather me, man.
The pieces I am, she gather them and give them back
to me in all the right order. It's good, you know, when you got a woman who is a friend of your mind.
[Toni Morrison, 1931–]

If you can eat today,
Enjoy the sunlight today,
Mix good cheer with friends today
Enjoy it,
And bless God for it.
[Henry Ward Beecher, 1813–1887]

THREE DELIGHTFUL LUNCHEONS

Grilled Chicken and Wild Rice Salad
Heirloom Tomato Soup
Coffee Mousse

Sockeye Salmon Mousse
Vegetables with Dill Dressing
Strawberry Fluff

CC's Turkey Casserole
Sea Island Salad
Fallen Praline Bars

The soul of Jonathan was
knit to the soul of David,
and Jonathan loved him as his own soul.
[1 Samuel 18:1]

Friendship is a single soul dwelling in two bodies.
[Aristotle, 322 BC]

There is one friend in the life of each
of us who seems not a separate person,
however dear and beloved, but an expansion,
an interpretation of one's self,
the very meaning of one's soul.
[Edith Wharton, 1862–1937]

GRILLED CHICKEN AND WILD RICE SALAD

Serves 6 to 8

Salad

1 pound boneless, skinless chicken breasts

1 (15-ounce) can apricot halves, drained

1 (8-ounce) package cultivated wild rice, cooked according to package directions

1/2 cup long-grain white rice, cooked according to package directions

1 (11-ounce) can mandarin oranges, drained

3/4 cup dried cranberries

1/2 cup chopped fresh parsley

1 cup sliced almonds, toasted

Vinaigrette

3 tablespoons red balsamic vinegar

1/4 cup orange juice

2 teaspoons Dijon mustard

3 tablespoons finely minced shallots

1/2 cup extra virgin olive oil

1 teaspoon sea salt

pepper to taste

For the salad: Place the chicken between two pieces of wax paper and pound to 1/4-inch thickness.

Preheat the grill to medium-high heat. Grill the chicken until no longer pink. Remove from the grill and slice into thin strips. Slice the apricots halves into three pieces each. Combine the chicken, apricots, wild rice, white rice, mandarin oranges, and cranberries.

For the vinaigrette: In a medium bowl combine the vinegar, orange juice, mustard, and shallots. Whisk in the olive oil, salt, and pepper. Toss the salad with enough dressing to moisten thoroughly. Refrigerate until chilled. Refrigerate the remaining dressing.

To serve: Toss the salad with a little more dressing and top with parsley and toasted almonds.

But friendship is precious, not only in the shade
but in the sunshine of life, and
thanks to benevolent arrangement, the greater part of life is sunshine.
[Thomas Jefferson, 1743–1826]

HEIRLOOM TOMATO SOUP

This soup is delicious served hot or cold.

Serves 6 to 8

2 tablespoons butter
1 medium onion, chopped
1 1/2 pounds fresh heirloom tomatoes, peeled and chopped
1 tablespoon minced fresh thyme
1/4 cup chopped fresh basil leaves
1/2 teaspoon granulated sugar
3 tablespoons tomato paste
1 1/2 cups chicken broth
1/2 cup half-and-half
salt and pepper to taste
1/2 cup grated Parmesan cheese

In a large saucepan on medium heat, melt the butter and add the onion. Sauté until tender. Add the tomatoes, thyme, basil, sugar, tomato paste, and chicken broth. Simmer about 30 minutes, until tender. Remove from the heat and puree in a blender or food processor in batches. Stir in the half-and-half, salt, and pepper. Add the Parmesan cheese and serve hot.

Note: This soup only gets better after a night in the refrigerator. Serve it cold for a refreshing lunchtime treat.

In the sweetness of friendship let there be laughter,
and sharing of pleasures.
For in the dew of little things the heart finds its morning and is refreshed.
[Kahlil Gibran, 1883–1931]

Our mouths were filled with laughter,
our tongues with songs of joy.
[Psalm 126:2 (NIV)]

COFFEE MOUSSE

Serves 4 to 6

1 cup heavy whipping cream
1 teaspoon instant coffee powder
1/4 cup strong-brewed coffee, chilled
2 tablespoons plus 2 teaspoons sugar
1 teaspoon vanilla
1 egg white at room temperature
whipped cream, for garnish
chocolate-covered coffee beans, for garnish

Chill a medium stainless steel bowl and beaters until cold. Place the cream and coffee powder in the bowl and beat until soft peaks form. Add the brewed coffee, two tablespoons sugar, and vanilla. Beat until stiff peaks form.

In a small copper or stainless steel bowl, beat the egg white until soft peaks form. Gradually add 2 teaspoons sugar and beat until stiff peaks form. Fold the egg white into the whipped cream mixture. Transfer to individual dessert bowls, cover, and chill several hours or overnight.

Garnish with whipped cream and chocolate-covered coffee beans.

The Three Fruits of Friendship

In 1625, the year before he died, Francis Bacon wrote an essay with this title. To the age-old thought that a friend "redoubleth joys and cutteth griefs in halves," he adds a second benefit of friendship that is sage advice: "The light that a man receiveth by counsel from another is dryer and purer than that which cometh from his own understanding." The third "fruit" is the outright aid that a friend offers "in all actions and occasions." He joyfully concludes with the observation that although we cannot "allege our own merits," the admirable things that we do are certainly "graceful in a friend's mouth"!

Friendship is a sheltering tree.
[Samuel Taylor Coleridge, 1772–1834]

SOCKEYE SALMON MOUSSE

Serves 6 to 8

2 (7 1/2-ounce) cans red sockeye salmon

2 (1/4-ounce) packages unflavored gelatin

1/4 cup chopped fresh parsley

1/2 cup chopped sweet onion (such as Vidalia)

1 cup chopped celery

1/2 cup chopped red bell pepper

1 cup mayonnaise

1 tablespoon Dijon mustard

1 tablespoon lemon juice

1/2 teaspoon Worcestershire sauce

1 tablespoon minced fresh thyme

2 tablespoons minced fresh dill

1 teaspoon seasoned salt

Drain the liquid from the salmon into a 1-cup measure and add enough water to fill the cup. In a small saucepan place the unflavored gelatin and the salmon liquid. Stir to combine and heat slowly to dissolve. Remove from the heat and set aside to cool.

In a food processor bowl, place the parsley, onion, celery, and red bell pepper. Pulse until finely chopped. Remove the bones from the salmon and discard. Add the salmon to the food processor and pulse until lightly chopped. Pour the mixture into a medium bowl and add the mayonnaise, mustard, lemon juice, Worcestershire sauce, thyme, dill, and salt. Stir in the dissolved gelatin and blend well.

Grease a 4-cup mold. Fill the mold with the salmon mousse and refrigerate for several hours or overnight. Serve with vegetables with dill dressing (page 50).

How fair doth Nature appear again!
How bright the sunbeams! How smiles the plain!
The flow'rs are bursting from ev'ry bough
A thousand voices each bush yields now.
And joy and gladness fill every breast!
Oh earth—Oh sunlight—Oh rapture blest.
[Johann Wolfgang von Goethe, 1749–1832]

VEGETABLES WITH DILL DRESSING

Makes 2 1/2 cups of dressing

Dill Dressing

2/3 cup mayonnaise

2/3 cup sour cream

1 tablespoon minced fresh dill

1 teaspoon lemon juice

1/2 cup buttermilk

Vegetables

1 1/2 pounds tender green beans cut into bite-size pieces

1 (14.5-ounce) can artichoke quarters, drained

1 (14.5-ounce) can hearts of palm, drained and cut into pieces

1 pint container grape tomatoes, halved

butterhead or Boston lettuce to line serving platter

For the dressing: In a small bowl mix the mayonnaise and sour cream together until blended. Stir in the dill, lemon juice, and buttermilk. Refrigerate until ready to serve.

For the vegetables: Fill a large bowl with water and ice. Set aside. Bring a large pot of water to a boil. Add the beans and cook until crisp-tender, 3 to 4 minutes. Drain the beans and place in the ice water to stop the cooking. Drain on paper towels. In a large bowl, combine the beans, artichoke quarters, hearts of palm, and tomatoes.

To assemble the meal: Place the lettuce on a large round serving platter. Unmold the salmon mousse (page 49) on the lettuce and surround with the vegetables. Serve with the dill dressing.

This visible world is wonderfully to be delighted in,
and highly to be esteemed, because it is the theatre of God's righteous Kingdom.
[Thomas Traherne, 1636–1674]

I have come to my garden . . .
Eat, O friends!
Drink, yes, drink deeply,
O beloved ones!
[Song of Solomon 5:1]

STRAWBERRY FLUFF

This is the perfect light dessert for a summer day.

Serves 10 to 12

5 cups fresh strawberries, hulled and washed, divided
1/3 cup granulated sugar
1/3 cup orange juice
juice of one lemon
2 (1/4-ounce) envelopes unflavored gelatin
1/2 cup hot water
2 cups heavy whipping cream

In a food processor or blender, puree four cups of the strawberries with the sugar. Place the mixture in a large bowl and stir in the orange and lemon juices. Set aside.

Stir the gelatin into the hot water until dissolved. Add to the strawberry mixture.

Whip the cream until soft peaks form. Save one cup of the whipped cream for garnish. Fold the remaining cream into the strawberry mixture. Place in a glass serving bowl. When ready to serve, top with the reserved whipped cream and strawberries.

Best friend, my wellspring in the wilderness.
[George Eliot, 1819–1880]

CC's Turkey Casserole

A great way to use that leftover holiday turkey.

Serves 10 to 12

2 tablespoons plus 1/3 cup butter

5 green onions, chopped

8 ounces sliced mushrooms

2 stalks celery, diced

1/3 cup all-purpose flour

2 cups half-and-half

1 1/2 cups milk

1/3 cup chicken broth

1/2 cup shredded sharp cheddar cheese

1/2 cup shredded Parmesan cheese

juice of one lemon

1 tablespoon dry mustard

2 tablespoons minced fresh parsley

salt and pepper to taste

4 cups chopped cooked turkey

3/4 pound spaghetti, cooked and drained

1/2 cup breadcrumbs

Preheat the oven to 350 degrees. In a saucepan melt 2 tablespoons butter over medium heat and sauté the onions, mushrooms, and celery until tender.

In a 4-quart saucepan, melt the 1/3 cup of butter over medium heat. Add the flour and stir for 1 minute. Remove the pan from the heat and stir in the half-and-half, milk, and chicken broth until well blended. Return the pan to the heat and cook, stirring constantly, until thickened. Stir in the cheddar cheese, Parmesan cheese, lemon juice, dry mustard, and parsley. Season to taste with salt and pepper.

Stir in the vegetable mixture, turkey, and cooked spaghetti. Place the mixture in a 3-quart casserole and top with the breadcrumbs. Bake for about 30 minutes until hot and bubbly.

Note: This dish can be prepared in the casserole dish and frozen, uncooked. Remove from the freezer and allow to sit on the counter while you preheat the oven, or thaw it in the refrigerator. If baking frozen increase baking time to 45 to 50 minutes.

It's not so much our friends help

that helps us as it is the confidence of their help.

[Epicurus, 341–270 BC]

SEA ISLAND SALAD

Serves 8 to 10

Red Wine Vinaigrette
1/2 cup red wine vinegar
2 cloves garlic, minced
2 teaspoons Worcestershire sauce
1 cup canola oil
salt and cracked pepper to taste

Salad
4 hearts Romaine lettuce, torn into bite-size pieces (about 8 to 10 cups)
1/2 cup grated Parmesan cheese
2 ounces crumbled blue cheese
garlic croutons

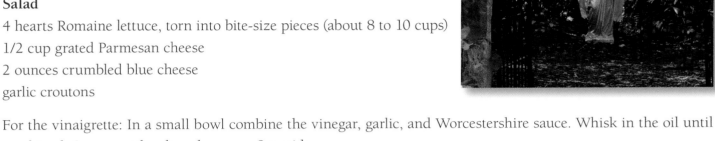

For the vinaigrette: In a small bowl combine the vinegar, garlic, and Worcestershire sauce. Whisk in the oil until combined. Season with salt and pepper. Set aside.

For the salad: Place the lettuce in a salad bowl and top with the cheeses and croutons. Toss with the dressing just before serving.

Give beauty back, beauty, beauty, beauty,
Back to God, beauty's self and beauty's giver.
[Gerard Manly Hopkins, 1844–1889]

"She calls her friends and neighbors together, saying, 'Rejoice with me . . .'"
[Luke 15:9]

They will celebrate your abundant goodness and joyfully sing of your righteousness.
[Psalm 145:7 (NIV)]

FALLEN PRALINE BARS

Rich and gooey!

Serves 12

1/2 cup unsalted butter, softened
1 (16-ounce) box light brown sugar
1 cup all-purpose flour
1 teaspoon baking soda
1 1/2 teaspoons vanilla
1 teaspoon salt
4 eggs
1 1/2 cups toffee bits
1 pint vanilla ice cream
butterscotch sauce to taste

Preheat the oven to 375 degrees. Grease and flour a 9 x 13-inch baking pan.

Place the butter and brown sugar in a large mixing bowl. With an electric mixer, cream the butter and brown sugar together until smooth. Add the flour, baking soda, vanilla, and salt. Add the eggs one at a time, mixing well after each addition. Stir in the toffee bits. Pour into the pan and bake for 20 to 25 minutes. Cool a few minutes and cut into 12 squares.

Serve warm topped with ice cream and butterscotch sauce.

Noonshine

Prior to the eighteenth century, when breakfast was typically eaten late and dinner early, this midday repast of bread and ale was enjoyed only by hardworking peasants. The word itself was considered too common to print! Jane Austen's unique reference to its derivative *nuncheon* helped it gain some degree of respectability and earned it the designation of *hapax legomenon*, which is a term applied to words used in any literary form "only once." Oddly, today's standard *lunch* is not a shortened form of what eventually came to be called *luncheon* but rather traces its own semantic origins to those early hearty laborers who took to the field each day only what they could *clunch* in their hands.

The plans I have for you

[Jeremiah 29:11 (NIV)]

FESTIVE OCCASIONS

We mutually as a family implore thy most special blessings upon one another.
We are brought into this close union by good Providence;
Grant that we may be fellow helpers to each other's faith, provoke each other to good works,
And encourage each other to run with alacrity the heavenward race.
May nearness to each other on earth lead to nearness in the eternal home.
Smile on the hearty desires of this domestic circle;
Bless us now and forevermore for Thy mercy's sake in Jesus Christ our Lord, Amen.
[*Family Prayers,* Henry Law, 1797–1884]

As this new chapter opens in reverent invocation, we eagerly anticipate that you might employ the same magnificent words to entreat God's blessing upon your next family gathering. What follows is a visual and culinary celebration of new chapters and important milestones. In honor of such events, we have brought out our finest accessories. We hope that you will enjoy seeing bright new accoutrements set happily alongside age-worn heirlooms and will be encouraged to use the things you have to tell your own family stories.

That these days should be remembered and kept throughout every generation, every family.
[Esther 9:28]

Suggestions for baptisms, confirmations, graduations, marriages, and retirements . . . all are here. We also have included a salute to the bravery of those who have chosen to lead a life of dedication to our country. And although the emphasis is not on established holidays, a tiny crèche lies ensconced as a gentle reminder that every event in Christian life is contingent upon one very particular birthday.

A third-century bishop of Carthage, Thacius Caecilius Cyprianus, St. Cyprian, once offered the most precious suggestion: that we should kiss babies at the moment of baptism "as if to catch a glimpse of God in the very act of creation." This creative process never stops but continues through every stage of life. From the delight of those who begat a child in Proverbs 23:24 to old age and even to gray hairs of Isaiah 46:4, every milestone represents, in a literal sense of the word, a thousand steps, all of which deserve applause. They give us opportunity to say, in the words of the beloved Dr. Seuss,

Today you are you that is truer than true.
There is no one alive who is youer than you!
[Theodore Seuss Geisel, 1904–1991]

Such happy events as are our subjects here need not be bound by traditional family ties. People with smaller families have opportunity to form new communities of affection and friendship based on adoption as children of God "for whom the whole family in heaven and earth is named" [Ephesians 3:15]. Whatever your family dynamic, we sincerely hope that the following pages will help you make every joyous celebration one of thanksgiving and praise to the Lord for the hospitality that He extends to us every day.

FESTIVE OCCASIONS

Marinated Dijon Shrimp

Walnut Cheese Wafers

Chicken Tarts

Hot Sausage Dip

Country Terrine

Spicy Herbed Hummus

Baked Crayfish Dip

Party Potato Wedges

Avocado, Tomato, and Feta Dip

Poulet Niçoise

Each of us is called to a special place in the Kingdom. If we find that place we will be happy. If we do not find it, we can never be completely happy. For each one of us there is only one thing necessary: . . . to be what God wants us to be.
[Thomas Merton, 1915–1968]

MARINATED DIJON SHRIMP

Always use the freshest shrimp for a fabulous treat!

Serves 6 to 8

1/4 cup Dijon mustard
1 teaspoon lemon juice
1/4 cup white wine vinegar
1/2 teaspoon salt
1/2 teaspoon pepper
1/2 cup extra virgin olive oil
1/4 cup finely chopped shallots
1 tablespoon chopped fresh dill
2 tablespoons chopped fresh chives
1/4 cup fresh chopped parsley
1 teaspoon dried oregano
1 1/2 pounds medium shrimp, peeled and cooked

In a blender or food processor, mix together the mustard, lemon juice, vinegar, salt, and pepper. Add the oil slowly while pulsing. Add the shallots, dill, chives, parsley, and oregano and pulse a few times to combine.

Place the shrimp in a serving bowl and pour the marinade over the shrimp. Chill for several hours before serving.

In all of us there is a hunger, marrow-deep,
to know our heritage—
to know who we are and where we come from.

In every conceivable manner, the family is link to our past, bridge to our future.
[*Roots*, Alex Haley, 1921–1992]

WALNUT CHEESE WAFERS

These are perfect little pick-up bites.

Makes 100

1/4 pound Fontina cheese, grated
1/2 cup butter, softened
1 1/2 cups all-purpose flour
1/2 teaspoon salt
dash of red pepper
1/3 cup chopped walnuts

In a food processor combine the cheese and butter until mixed. In a small bowl sift the flour, salt, and pepper together and add to the cheese mixture. Pulse until it forms a ball on the blade. Remove from the processor, place in a medium bowl, and combine with the walnuts. Divide the dough into two parts. Roll each part into a long roll about the diameter of a quarter and wrap tightly in wax paper. Place in the refrigerator at least an hour to allow the dough to firm up. Preheat the oven to 300 degrees.

Slice into 1/4-inch slices and place 1 inch apart on a cookie sheet. Bake 20 to 25 minutes until golden brown. Remove to a cooling rack.

Note: Freezes beautifully.

Now therefore, let it please

You to bless the house of Your servant, that it may continue before You forever; for You, O Lord God, have spoken it, and with Your blessing let the house of Your servant be blessed forever.
[2 Samuel 7:29]

I will bless you . . .
And you shall be a blessing.
And in you all the families of the earth shall be blessed.
[Genesis 12:2–3]

When families are to be built up,
He is the founder of them.
[Matthew Henry, 1662–1714]

CHICKEN TARTS

Makes 60 small tarts

4 cups finely chopped cooked chicken

2/3 cup mayonnaise

2 tablespoons Heinz 57 sauce

3/4 teaspoon curry powder

1/2 teaspoon seasoned salt

cayenne pepper to taste

2 stalks celery, very finely chopped

60 small tart shells

1 cup toasted slivered almonds, chopped, for garnish

Combine the chicken, mayonnaise, Heinz 57 sauce, curry powder, seasoned salt, and pepper in the bowl of a food processor and pulse until mixed well but still chunky. Add the celery and pulse 2 or 3 times to mix. Remove to a bowl and chill several hours or overnight.

To serve, fill the tart shells with the chicken mixture and sprinkle the toasted almonds on top for garnish.

Oh, there is power in a mother's trust.
As surely as Moses was put in his mother's arms by the princess,
so God puts babes in your arms, as
a charge by Him to raise and care for. That is a jewel that belongs to God
and He gives it to you to polish for Him so He can set it in a crown.
[Billy Sunday, 1862–1935]

Rejoice with your family in the beautiful land of life.
[Albert Einstein, 1879–1955]

'Tis sufficient to say, according to the proverb,
that here is God's plenty.
[John Dryden, 1631–1700]

Listen carefully to Me, and eat what is good,
And let your soul delight itself in abundance.
[Isaiah 55:2]

Hot Sausage Dip

Men love this!

Serves 20

1 pound hot pork sausage
5 green onions, chopped with some green parts
1 Roma tomato, seeded and finely chopped
1 cup sour cream
1/2 cup real mayonnaise
1/4 cup grated Parmesan cheese
1/2 cup shredded mozzarella cheese
corn chips, for dipping

Preheat oven to 350 degrees.

In a small skillet break up the sausage into small pieces and cook until browned. Drain and combine with the onions, tomato, sour cream, mayonnaise, Parmesan cheese, and mozzarella cheese. Place in a 4-cup baking dish and bake 20 to 25 minutes until hot and bubbly. Serve with corn chips.

The father of the righteous will greatly rejoice,
And he who begets a child will delight in him.
Let your father and your mother be glad,
And let her who bore you rejoice.
[Proverbs 23:24–25]

Oh God, we can trust you and we do.
Our faith has gathered strength by the lapse of years.
Each following birthday, we trust, confirms us in the fact that to rely on God
is our strength and our happiness.
[Charles Spurgeon, 1834–1892]

COUNTRY TERRINE

Serves 12 to 15

1/2 pound hot Italian sausage
1 pound mild Italian sausage
1 1/2 pounds chicken livers
1/2 cup chopped yellow onion
1/3 cup all-purpose flour
1/4 cup brandy, optional
1 teaspoon salt
1/2 teaspoon ground allspice
1/4 teaspoon ground nutmeg
1/4 teaspoon ground cloves
2 garlic cloves, minced
3 eggs
cracked pepper to taste
4 thinly sliced green onions with some green parts
1/2 cup small capers
1 pound lean bacon
cornichons, olives, and toast points for serving

Preheat the oven to 350 degrees.

In a medium skillet break up the sausage in small bits and cook until browned. In the bowl of a food processor, place the chicken livers, onion, flour, brandy, salt, allspice, nutmeg, cloves, garlic, eggs, and cracked pepper and pulse until well mixed. Add the green onions and capers and pulse a couple more times to mix. Line a 5-cup terrine mold with the bacon, extending the ends over the sides. Add the sausage to the liver mixture and spoon into the mold. Fold the bacon ends back over the top. Cover tightly with foil and place in a pan filled with 1/2 inch of hot water. Bake at 350 degrees for 1 1/2 hours.

Remove from the oven and place weights on top of the terrine (soup cans work fine) and refrigerate for at least 6 hours or overnight. Unmold and serve with cornichons, olives, and toast points.

You don't choose your family.
They are God's gift to you as you are to them.
[Desmond Tutu, 1984 Nobel Peace Prize, 1931–]

SPICY HERBED HUMMUS

Serves 10 to 12

2 (14.5-ounce) cans chickpeas, drained and rinsed

2 tablespoons tahini paste

2 cloves garlic, minced

juice of two lemons

3 to 4 tablespoons extra virgin olive oil

1 teaspoon ground cumin

1 heaping teaspoon dried oregano

1 teaspoon dried basil

1 teaspoon dried thyme

1 teaspoon sea salt

dash hot sauce, optional

pita chips and assorted vegetables, for dipping

Combine the chickpeas, tahini, garlic, lemon juice, 3 tablespoons olive oil, cumin, oregano, basil, thyme, salt, and hot sauce in the bowl of a food processor and pulse into a smooth paste. Add the last tablespoon of olive oil if it is too thick.

Refrigerate several hours before serving.

A feast is made for laughter.
[Ecclesiastes 10:19]

But he who is of a merry heart has a continual feast.
[Proverbs 15:15]

So this day shall be to you a memorial;
and you shall keep it as a feast to the LORD throughout your generations.
[Exodus 12:14]

BAKED CRAYFISH DIP

Serves 16 to 20

4 tablespoons butter

1 large mild yellow onion, finely chopped

6 green onions, chopped (bottoms and 2 inches of green parts)

2 cloves garlic, minced

2 cups cream cheese, cut into cubes

1 pound frozen, peeled crayfish, thawed, drained, and chopped roughly

Cajun seasoning to taste

salt, pepper, and hot sauce to taste

1 red bell pepper, roasted and diced

1/4 cup chopped fresh parsley

corn chips, for dipping

In a small pan melt the butter over medium heat. Sauté the onions and garlic until tender. Stir the cheese into the vegetables until melted. Add the crayfish and season with the Cajun seasoning and salt and pepper to taste. Add hot sauce to taste. Stir in the red bell pepper and parsley. Place in the refrigerator for several hours for the flavors to blend.

Preheat the oven to 350 degrees and bake until hot and bubbly, about 30 minutes. Serve with corn chips for dipping.

I have come home at last!
This is my real country! I belong here. I have been looking for this land all of my life,
although I never knew it until now.
[*The Last Battle*, C. S. Lewis, 1898–1963]

I'll pray you grow up to be a brave man in a brave country.
I will pray you find a way to be useful. I'll pray and then I'll sleep.
[Marilynne Robinson, 1943–]

Party Potato Wedges

So easy and always a hit.

Serves 12 to 15

5 small Russet potatoes, unpeeled (about 4 inches long each)
vegetable oil (about 1/3 cup)
seasoned salt to taste (about 1 teaspoon)
cracked pepper to taste (about 1 teaspoon)
1 teaspoon paprika

Preheat the oven to 425 degrees. Slice each potato into small wedges, 8 to 10 per potato. Place the potatoes in a large bowl and sprinkle generously with the oil. Stir to evenly coat each potato. Place on a large jellyroll pan and sprinkle with the seasoned salt, cracked pepper, and paprika. Bake 30 to 40 minutes, until tender and beginning to brown, turning frequently.

Serve immediately or allow to rest and reheat just before serving.

Place your favorite dip in the center of a large serving tray and surround with the warm potatoes.

Note: These are especially good with a bacon ranch or cheesy onion dip.

And after eating splendid foods, having cleared the tables,
we played and sang many songs and enjoyed graceful and beautiful dances.
[*Il Paradiso degli Alberti*, Giovani Gherardi da Prato, 1426–]

So they ate and drank before the LORD with great gladness on that day.
[1 Chronicles 29:22]

Avocado, Tomato, and Feta Dip

Serves 12 to 15

4 Haas avocados, diced

juice of one lime

2 garlic cloves, minced

1 teaspoon cumin

1 teaspoon dried oregano

2 cups grape tomatoes, drained and quartered

1/2 medium red onion, diced

1/2 cup crumbled Feta cheese

1/4 cup red wine vinegar

1/4 cup extra virgin olive oil

salt and pepper to taste

assorted Greek olives, for garnish

tortilla chips, for dipping

In a medium bowl combine the avocados and lime juice. Add the garlic, cumin, oregano, tomatoes, onion, Feta cheese, vinegar, and oil. Taste for salt and pepper. Garnish with olives. Serve with tortilla chips for dipping.

My, my, my, I'm so happy,
I'm gonna join the band,
We are gonna dance and sing
in celebration,
we are in the promised land.
[Led Zeppelin]

Also with the lute I will praise You-
And Your faithfulness, O my God!
To You I will sing with the harp,
O Holy One of Israel.
[Psalm 71:22]

Poulet Niçoise

Delicious!

Serves 25

4 boneless, skinless chicken breast halves, poached and
   cut into bite-size pieces
1 cup pitted Nicoise olives, drained
1 (8.5-ounce) can quartered artichoke hearts, drained
1 pound button mushrooms
1/3 cup red wine vinegar
1/3 cup Dijon mustard
1 teaspoon sea salt
cracked pepper to taste
1 teaspoon dried tarragon (1 tablespoon minced fresh)
1 teaspoon dried oregano (1 tablespoon minced fresh)
3/4 cup extra virgin olive oil
leaf lettuce, for serving

Place the chicken, olives, artichokes, and mushrooms in a large mixing bowl.

In a small bowl whisk together the vinegar, mustard, sea salt, pepper, tarragon, and oregano. While whisking, slowly add the olive oil until emulsified.

Pour the vinaigrette over the chicken mixture and stir gently to coat. Refrigerate several hours to allow the flavors to blend. Line a serving platter with lettuce and cover with the chicken mixture. Serve with toothpicks.

A man's heart plans his way,
But the Lord directs his steps.
[Proverbs 16:9]

'Tis sweeter far to me . . .

To walk together to the kirk,
And all together pray,
While each to his great Father bends,
Old men, and babes, and loving friends.

He prayeth best who loveth best
All things both great and small;
For the dear God who loveth us,
He made and loveth all.
[*The Rime of the Ancient Mariner*, Samuel Taylor Coleridge, 1772–1834]

"And you welcomed me"
[Matthew 25:35 (ESV)]

FOUR CONVIVIAL DINNERS

We now stand ready to open our doors with warm welcoming for those who are newcomers in our neighborhoods, schools, churches, and places of work. According to Corrie Ten Boom, the heroic Dutch woman who sheltered in her home hundreds of the persecuted during the Second World War, "every experience that God gives us, every person that He puts in our lives is the perfect preparation for the future that only He can see"

No one knew this better than the earliest believers. Their commitment to hospitality gave them a unique identity and facilitated the rapid growth of Christian faith. One of the earliest writings about them found outside of the Bible describes the phenomenon:

> And when they [the Christians] see the stranger, they bring him into their dwellings and rejoice over him as a true
> brother; for they do not call brothers those who are after the flesh, but those who are in the spirit and in God. They
> do good to those who are their neighbors. And because they acknowledge the goodness of God toward them, lo! on
> account of them there flows forth the beauty that is in the world. And truly this people is a new people, and there is
> something divine mingled with it.
> [*The Apology*, Aristides, fl. second century]

As proud inheritors of such a legacy, it becomes a holy joy to ensure that such practices remain a part of the Christian ethos. Can we, like them, find in every hospitable transaction a measure of Christology, ecclesiology, and eschatology? Might every guest become the potential means by which we might imitate Christ, share the spirit of His church, and in some measure foreshadow the feast of the eternal kingdom. In New Testament Greek, the words *host*, *guest*, and *stranger* are interrelated as *xenos*. Hospitality thus becomes a relationship, a natural reflection of Christ, the archetypical wanderer who is simultaneously God's chief householder. Delight in the entire guest-host relationship is known as *philoxenia*. For Christians this delight is fuelled by the expectation that the Holy Spirit will always be present at the table.

We conclude with the inspiration of an almost forgotten Ohio poetess who counted among her friends the likes of Edgar Allen Poe, John Greenleaf Whittier, and P. T. Barnum. She was as well known for the lavish hospitality of her New York dinner parties as she was for her literary achievements.

NOBILITY
True worth is in being, not seeming
In doing, each day that goes by,
Some little good—not in dreaming of great things to do by and by.
For whatever men say in their blindness, and in spite of the fancies of youth,
There's nothing so kingly as kindness, and nothing so royal as truth.
[Alice Carey, 1820–1871]

If there is any concept worth restoring to its original depth
and evocative potential, it is the concept of hospitality.
[Henri J.M. Nouwen, 1932–1996]

FOUR CONVIVIAL DINNERS

Sunday Rib Roast
Potatoes Annette
Roasted Beet and Carrot Salad

Spicy Sausage and Chicken Lasagna
Bacon and Blue Cheese Salad

Finley's Baby Back Ribs
Summer Succotash
Orange Kiwi Salad

Crabmeat Almandine
Portobello and Roasted Red Pepper Salad
Chocolate Coffee Pie

If we really want to learn
to love others, we must first begin to love one another in
our own home . . . from here, from our own home, love
will spread to my neighbor,
in the street where I live, in the town where I live,
in the whole world.
[Mother Teresa, Agnes Gonxha Bojaxhiu, 1910–1997]

Sunday Rib Roast

The slow cooking makes this roast tender and very juicy.

Serves 6 to 8

1 3-rib beef roast (preferably first-cut)
all-purpose flour, for coating
sea salt
cracked black pepper
8 whole garlic cloves, peeled

Preheat oven to 250 degrees.

Tie the roast in three spots around the bones. Sprinkle the roast lightly with flour. Season with salt and pepper. In a large roasting pan, place the roast fat side down and cook over a medium-high burner (you may need two burners) until well browned. Turn to brown the other sides. Turn fat side up, and with a sharp knife, pierce the fat about one inch down in eight places evenly spaced across the top of the roast. Push a whole garlic clove into each cut spot. Remove the roast from the pan. Place a wire roasting rack in the pan and place the roast on the rack.

Place the roast in the oven and cook 30 minutes for each pound for medium-rare, or until the meat registers 130 degrees on a meat thermometer. Let rest for several minutes before carving.

Note: Remove the roast from the refrigerator a couple of hours before cooking so it cooks evenly.

What is pleasanter than the tie of host and guest.
[*The Libation Bearers*, Aeschylus, 525–455 BC]

Now when he had brought them into his house, he set food before them;
and he rejoiced, having believed in God with all his household.
[Acts 16:34]

POTATOES ANNETTE

Serves 10 to 12

4 tablespoons butter, divided
3 tablespoons all-purpose flour
1/2 cup chicken broth
1/2 cup milk
1/2 teaspoon salt
cracked black pepper to taste
3 pounds Idaho potatoes, peeled and cooked until tender
2 cups sour cream
2 cups grated New York extra-sharp cheddar cheese
4 green onions, sliced, some green parts
1 1/2 cups crushed corn flakes

Preheat the oven to 350 degrees.

In a small skillet melt one tablespoon of butter over medium heat. Add the flour and stir for one minute. Remove the pan from the heat and stir in the chicken broth and milk until well blended. Return the pan to the heat and cook, stirring constantly, until thickened. Add the salt and pepper and remove from the heat.

In a large bowl combine the milk sauce, potatoes, sour cream, cheese, and green onions. Place the mixture in a 3-quart casserole, top with the crushed corn flakes, and dot with the remaining 3 tablespoons of butter. Bake for 30 minutes until bubbly and hot throughout.

Note: You can prepare the dish ahead of time and refrigerate. Top with the corn flakes just before baking and add 30 minutes to the cooking time.

"The kingdom of heaven is like a householder who brings
out of his treasure things new and old."
[Matthew 13:52]

Guide your guests around the house and in particular show them some of your possessions, either new or beautiful, but in such a way that it will be received as a sign of your politeness and domesticity, and not arrogance: something that you will do as if showing them your heart.
[*Institutione della sposa, A Handbook for New Brides, 1587,* Pietro Belmonte]

And the natives showed us unusual kindness; for they kindled a fire and made us all welcome.
[Acts 28:2]

Roasted Beet and Carrot Salad

Serves 6 to 8

Dressing

1/4 cup balsamic vinegar

2 tablespoons lemon juice

2 teaspoons soy sauce

1 teaspoon granulated sugar

2 garlic cloves, minced

1 teaspoon sea salt

cracked black pepper to taste

1/4 cup extra virgin olive oil

Salad

3 medium beets, cleaned and trimmed (about a pound)

canola oil, for drizzling

1/3 pound baby carrots, halved

sea salt

8 cups baby arugula or mixed baby lettuces

1 cup crumbled goat cheese

1/2 cup toasted pine nuts

To make the dressing: Combine the vinegar, lemon juice, soy sauce, sugar, garlic, sea salt, and pepper in a small bowl. Whisk in the olive oil to blend. Set aside.

To make the salad: Preheat the oven to 400 degrees. Place the beets on a piece of heavy-duty aluminum foil and drizzle with a little oil. Fold the foil up over the beets and seal to keep from leaking. Place in the oven and bake until tender and easy to peel. Start checking at thirty minutes, but they make take as long as an hour.

When cool, peel the skin and cut the beets in half. Slice the halves into bite-size pieces. Refrigerate. In a small bowl, toss the carrots with a little oil to coat and place on a baking sheet. Sprinkle lightly with sea salt. Place in the oven and roast until tender. Check after 20 minutes. Refrigerate.

To serve, place the arugula in a salad bowl. Top with the beets, carrots, goat cheese, and pine nuts. Toss with the dressing.

Note: Wear rubber gloves when handling the beets to avoid staining your hands.

A guest comes to share not only meat, wine, and dessert, but
conversation, fun, and the amiability that leads to friendship.
[Plutarch, AD 46–120]

SPICY SAUSAGE AND CHICKEN LASAGNA

This is a long recipe, but the results are worth all the effort. Prepare a day ahead and cook when the company arrives.

Serves 10 to 12

4 tablespoons olive oil, divided
1 pound sweet Italian sausage
1 (12-ounce) package sliced mushrooms
1 cup chopped green bell pepper
1 cup chopped celery
1 cup chopped white onion
2 garlic cloves, minced
3 tablespoons butter
4 tablespoons all-purpose flour
2 cups chicken broth
1 cup half-and-half
2 cups crushed tomatoes
3 cups cooked, chopped chicken
1 cup pitted sliced Kalamata olives
1 tablespoon Worcestershire sauce
salt and pepper to taste
Tabasco sauce to taste
1 (9-ounce) package no-boil lasagna (preferably Barilla)
3 cups grated New York sharp cheddar cheese, divided
1/2 cup grated Parmesan cheese

Preheat the oven to 375 degrees.

Heat 2 tablespoons of the olive oil in a large skillet. Remove the sausage from the casing and break into small pieces. Sauté the sausage in the oil until no longer pink. Remove the sausage from the pan and put on a plate. Sauté the mushrooms until they become limp. Remove the mushrooms from the pan and add to the sausage. Add the remaining 2 tablespoons of oil to the pan and sauté the bell pepper, celery, onion, and garlic until tender. Set aside.

In a 3-quart saucepan, melt the butter over medium heat and stir in the flour for 1 minute. Remove from the heat and stir in the chicken broth and half-and-half until well blended. Return to the heat and cook, stirring constantly until thickened. Stir in the sausage, mushrooms, vegetables, tomatoes, chicken, olives, and Worcestershire. Season with salt, pepper, and Tabasco sauce to taste.

Spread 1/3 of the sauce in the bottom of a 13 x 9 x 3-inch baking pan. Cover with 4 sheets of pasta. Spread 1/3 more sauce on the pasta and cover with 1/2 of the cheddar cheese. Cover with 4 more sheets of pasta and spread the remaining sauce on top. Sprinkle the top with the remaining cheddar and Parmesan cheeses. Bake 30 to 40 minutes until hot and bubbly.

Note: Make ahead and refrigerate. Before baking, bring to room temperature. Increase baking time to 50–60 minutes.

BACON AND BLUE CHEESE SALAD

Serves 6 to 8

Vinaigrette

2 tablespoons red wine vinegar

2 tablespoons balsamic vinegar

1 clove garlic, minced

1/2 teaspoon dry mustard

1 teaspoon granulated sugar

1 teaspoon sea salt

cracked black pepper

1/2 cup extra virgin olive oil

Salad

3/4 pound mixed lettuces

8 strips good quality bacon, cooked crisp and crumbled

4 ounces blue cheese (Maytag preferred)

1/2 cup honey-roasted pecans, optional

1 small red onion, sliced

To make the vinaigrette: In a small bowl whisk together the vinegars, garlic, mustard, sugar, salt, pepper, and olive oil.

To make the salad: Place the lettuce in a medium salad bowl. Top with the bacon, blue cheese, pecans, and red onion. Toss with the vinaigrette and serve immediately.

Wisdom has built her house . . .
She has also furnished her table.
She cries out from the highest places . . .

"Come, eat of my bread
and drink of the wine I have mixed . . .
And go in the way of understanding."
[Proverbs 9:1–6]

To thee, whose temple is all space,
Whose altar, earth, sea, skies!
One chorus let all being raise!
All Nature's incense rise!
[Alexander Pope, 1688–1744]

FINLEY'S BABY BACK RIBS

These are delicious and a snap to cook when the weather is bad.
You won't even miss the grill!

Serves 8 to 10

3 cups apple cider vinegar

1/2 cup honey

1 tablespoon Old Bay seasoning

1 tablespoon black pepper

1 tablespoon garlic salt

3 racks baby back ribs (6 to 7 pounds total)

Preheat the oven to 250 degrees.

In a small bowl mix the vinegar, honey, Old Bay, pepper, and garlic salt. Place the ribs, bone side down, in a large roasting pan. Baste with 1/3 of the sauce and cover tightly with aluminum foil. Bake for at least 6 hours, basting every hour. Check for doneness. Continue cooking and basting until they are browned and almost falling off the bone. This may take 3 or 4 more hours depending on the thickness of the ribs. Remove the ribs to a serving platter and pour the basting juice from the pan over the ribs.

Note: This slow-cooking method makes the ribs very juicy and tender. A disposable foil-roasting pan works great with this recipe.

Surely it is very pleasant to have so well furnished a house
that it will never be necessary to darken the parlour windows to whoever calls, and to set such a table as that
we shall not be ashamed to have any visitor suddenly drop in to try pot luck.
["Save a Little Something," *New York Daily Times*, April 18, 1855]

SUMMER SUCCOTASH

Wonderful in the summer when vegetables are at their peak of freshness.

Serves 8 to 10

2 tablespoons butter
1 large mild onion, chopped
2 large tomatoes, chopped, with juice
1 pound okra, sliced
2 cups corn, cut from cob
2 cups cooked butter beans
1 teaspoon Lawry's seasoned salt
cracked black pepper to taste

Melt the butter in a large Dutch oven and sauté the onion until tender.

Add the tomatoes and okra and cook until the okra is tender. Stir in the corn and butter beans and cook a few minutes for flavors to blend. Season with salt and pepper.

Note: This is even better cooked a day ahead and reheated.

For every house is built by someone,
but He who built all things is God.
[Hebrews 3:4]

ORANGE KIWI SALAD

Refreshing!

Serves 8 to 10

Dressing

4 tablespoons fresh orange juice

1 1/2 tablespoons red wine vinegar

1 teaspoon lemon juice

2 tablespoons granulated sugar

1 teaspoon sea salt

1/2 teaspoon dry mustard

1 garlic clove, minced

1/3 cup extra virgin olive oil

Salad

1 1/2 pounds baby Romaine lettuce, torn into bite-size pieces

3 kiwi fruit, peeled and sliced

1 (11-ounce) can mandarin oranges, drained

1/2 cup chopped green onions

1/3 cup toasted nuts, optional

To make the dressing: In a small bowl combine the orange juice, vinegar, lemon juice, sugar, salt, mustard, and garlic. Whisk in the olive oil until well combined.

To make the salad: In a large salad bowl, place the lettuce. Top with the kiwis, oranges, green onions, and nuts. Toss with the dressing just before serving.

"By this My Father is glorified,
that you bear much fruit; so you will be My disciples."
[John 15:8]

No one of this nation ever begs, for the houses of all are common to all;
and they consider liberality and hospitality the first virtues.
[Giraldus Cambrensis, 1146–1223]

CRABMEAT ALMANDINE

Best-quality crabmeat is the key to this recipe.

Serves 4

4 tablespoons butter, divided
2 tablespoons all-purpose flour
1 cup half-and-half
1 teaspoon Everglades all-purpose seasoning
1 tablespoon chili sauce
1/2 teaspoon Worcestershire sauce
juice of one lemon
1/2 teaspoon white pepper
1 teaspoon sea salt
1 pound fresh lump crabmeat
3/4 cup sliced almonds

Preheat the oven to 350 degrees.

In a medium saucepan melt 2 tablespoons butter over medium heat. Stir in the 2 tablespoons of flour. Remove the pan from the heat and stir in the half-and-half until well blended. Return the pan to the heat and cook, stirring constantly, until thickened. Remove from the heat and stir in the Everglades seasoning, chili sauce, Worcestershire sauce, lemon juice, pepper, salt, and crabmeat. Taste for salt and pepper.

In a small saucepan melt 2 tablespoons butter and stir in the sliced almonds. Remove from the heat.

Divide the crab mixture between 4 large scallop shells or individual ramekins. Top with the buttered almonds and bake until browned and bubbly, 15 to 20 minutes.

Note: Everglades seasoning is found in most grocery stores and is available online.

Love hospitality, whereby holy Abraham found favor,
and received Christ as his guest, and Sarah already worn with age received a son.
The spirit of hospitality should not fail at our table.
We should meet a guest with ready and free service and look out for his arrival.
[Ambrose of Milan, 339–397]

PORTOBELLO AND ROASTED RED PEPPER SALAD

Serves 6 to 8

Vinaigrette
1/4 cup balsamic vinegar
1 teaspoon dried oregano
1/2 teaspoon sea salt
freshly ground pepper
1/2 cup extra virgin olive oil

Salad
12 ounces sliced portobello mushrooms
1/4 cup extra virgin olive oil
12 ounces baby Romaine lettuce
2 roasted red bell peppers, sliced in strips
1 cup crumbled Feta cheese

To make the vinaigrette: In a small bowl whisk the vinegar with the oregano, sea salt, pepper, and 1/2 cup olive oil. Set aside.

To make the salad: Brush the portobellos with the olive oil and grill or sauté in a small preheated pan until tender, 3 to 5 minutes per side. Place the lettuce in a salad bowl and top with the mushrooms, red peppers, and Feta cheese. Toss with the vinaigrette to serve.

Emerson Entertains

A new person is a great event to me and hinders me from sleep . . . I awoke this morning with devout thanksgiving for my friends, the old and the new. Shall I not call God the Beautiful, who daily showeth Himself so to me in His gifts.

The house is dusted, all things fly into their places, the old coat is exchanged for the new, and they must get up a good dinner if they can. The guest stands to us for humanity.

'Tis good to give . . . a meal or a night's lodging. 'Tis better to be hospitable to his good meaning and thought, and give courage to a companion.
[Ralph Waldo Emerson, 1803–1882]

CHOCOLATE COFFEE PIE

Divine!

Serves 6 to 8

2 large eggs

1 cup granulated sugar

1/2 cup melted butter

1/4 cup strong brewed coffee

1/4 cup cornstarch

1 cup chopped pecans

1 cup semi-sweet chocolate bits

1 (9-inch) deep-dish pie shell, unbaked

Preheat the oven to 350 degrees.

With an electric mixer beat the eggs. Gradually add the sugar. Slowly beat in the butter, coffee, and cornstarch. Mix until the cornstarch is incorporated. Stir in the pecans and chocolate bits. Pour into the pie shell and bake for 45 to 50 minutes until set.

Serve warm with whipped cream or coffee ice cream.

That which we have seen and heard we declare to you,
that you may have fellowship with us; and truly our fellowship is with the Father and with His Son Jesus Christ. And these things we write to you that your joy may be full.
[1 John 1:3–4]

Until I declare
Your strength to this generation
[Psalm 71:18]

Hospitality for the Very Young

Please try to imagine this chapter as a conversation with tradition. We invite you not only to enter the dialogue but to actually preside over it. The purpose is to emphasize how important it is to teach our children the ways of hospitable living and at the same time to offer ourselves as role models. Some of the ideas that we have included may be helpful for teaching while others are for pleasing and serving your younger guests. We expect that the whimsical imagery of the following pages will lead you to fond recollections of your own halcyon days of childhood.

We give our children wings but if they never see us fly, how will they know how to use them?
[Hafiz, 1320–1389]

Authentic hospitality communicates to our guests the feeling that a place has been prepared especially for them. Color, texture, shape, taste, and smell all help convey this sensation. "Place cards" define it! As we joyfully prepare such places, we fly about setting everything aright. Participation in this experience gives observant children wings to follow. The hospitable activities of an older generation thus instill in a younger one both the desire and the means of welcoming others. C. S. Lewis maintained that attitudes are infectious. Do you agree? As a consolation for the happy confusion that often occurs when children are present, we can but smile upon the words of race car driver Mario Andretti, whose career spanned four decades: "If you're in control, you're probably not going fast enough!"

The New Testament opens with the genealogy of Jesus (Matthew 1:1–17) in which may be found numerous examples of hospitality being taught to the next generation. Rahab sheltered the spies, and her son Boaz opened his doors to Ruth. David invited Mephibosheth to dine with him continuously, and David's son Solomon consistently prepared a table of full supply. Some have gone so far as to suggest that Mary's gracious receiving of the baby Jesus into herself was hospitality personified. In this teaching Jesus found a holy and royal tradition that we are privileged to continue with our own families.

In the early days of Christianity, *traditores* were those who scornfully "handed over" their believing brethren to persecuting authorities. Fortunately, tradition took on positive form and became integral to Christian faith. It is best informed by Scripture. The law of Deuteronomy 4:9 is "teach them to your children and grandchildren," and the response to Psalm 92:14 is to "still bear fruit in old age." Psalm 71:18 is even more specific, adding "also when I am old and grayheaded." Jesus and later John's use of the term "little children" is an allegorical reference to all of us. It is a kind reminder that at every age we strive to live in ways more pleasing to our Father who has so generously prepared a place for us not just here on earth but forever. We hope that this conversation has helped you find in the tradition of hospitality a means of helping the young people in your life discern the pleasing and perfect place that God has prepared for each one of them.

What I really need is to get clear about what
I must do, not what I must know. . . .
What matters is to find a purpose, to see what it really is that God wills that I should do.
[Søren Kierkegaard, 1813–1855]

HOSPITALITY FOR THE VERY YOUNG

Aunt Emma's Tea Cakes

Creamy Cheddar Corn Chowder

Macaroni Cupcakes

Strawberry Fruit Dip

Honey Lemon Chicken Wing Drumettes

Country Apple Pie

Barbeque Meatballs

Fresh Berry Pizza

If a child is to keep
his inborn sense of wonder, he needs the companionship of at least one adult who can share it, rediscovering with him the joy, excitement and mystery of the world we live in.
[Rachael Carson, 1907–1964]

"Do you understand what you are reading?"
And he said, "How can I
unless someone guides me?"
[Acts 8:30–31]

AUNT EMMA'S TEA CAKES

Makes 15 to 20 large cookies

2 cups all-purpose flour
2 teaspoons baking powder
1/2 teaspoon salt
1/4 teaspoon grated nutmeg
1/2 cup unsalted butter, room temperature
1 cup granulated sugar
2 eggs, lightly beaten
1 teaspoon vanilla
crystallized sugar, for sprinkling

In a small bowl sift the flour, baking powder, salt, and nutmeg together. In a mixing bowl cream the butter until smooth and beat in the sugar, eggs, and vanilla. Stir in the flour mixture until well combined. Chill thoroughly.

Preheat the oven to 375 degrees. Roll dough to 1/4-inch thickness on a lightly floured board and cut with a floured 2 1/2-inch cookie cutter. Sprinkle with crystallized sugar, if desired. Place on a greased cookie sheet and bake for 8 to 10 minutes. Cool on a wire rack.

THE PRAYER OF THE LITTLE BIRD

Dear God,
I don't know how to pray by myself
very well,
but will you please
protect my little nest from wind and rain?
Put a great deal of dew on the flowers,
many seeds in my way.
Make Your blue very high,
your branches lissome;
let Your kind light stay late in the sky
and set my heart brimming with such music
that I must sing, sing, sing . . .
Please, Lord
[*Prayers from the Ark,* Carmen Bernos De Gasztold,
translated by Rumer Godden, 1907–1998]

CREAMY CHEDDAR CORN CHOWDER

Serves 4

2 tablespoons butter

1/2 cup finely minced mild onion, optional

2 tablespoons all-purpose flour

1 1/2 cups chicken broth

1 1/2 cups half-and-half

8 ounces sharp cheddar cheese, shredded (better to shred
   yourself)

1/3 cup crumbled crisp bacon (or Real Bacon Bits)

1 cup cream-style corn

salt to taste

In a 2-quart saucepan over medium heat, melt the butter. Add the onion and cook until tender. Stir in the flour and cook until well blended. Remove from the heat and add the chicken broth and half-and-half. Stir to combine well.

Return to the heat and stir in the cheese, bacon, and corn. Cook, uncovered, at least 15 minutes on low heat to thicken and combine flavors. Stir frequently. Taste for seasonings.

Imagine if you can what the rest of the evening was like.
How they crouched by the fire which blazed and made so much of itself in the little grate. How they removed the covers of the dishes and found rich, hot, savory soup, which was a meal in itself, and sandwiches and toast and muffins enough for both of them.
[*The Little Princess,* Frances Hodgson Burnett, 1849–1924]

As for children . . . let a kind consideration be shown to them,
and let them eat before the regular hours.
[St. Benedict, 480–547]

Macaroni Cupcakes

Serves 6

1 jumbo 6-cup muffin tin

vegetable cooking spray

1/2 cup Panko bread crumbs (or homemade crumbs)

1 1/2 cups small elbow macaroni
  (or your favorite small shape)

1 1/2 cups milk

2 teaspoons all-purpose flour

1 tablespoon butter, melted

2 eggs, beaten

1/2 teaspoon powdered mustard

1 teaspoon Lawry's seasoned salt

2 cups grated Jarlsburg or cheddar cheese

Preheat the oven to 350 degrees. Spray the muffin tins with cooking spray and coat the insides of the cups with the Panko crumbs.

Bring a large pot of water to a boil and cook the pasta until al dente (8 to 10 minutes). Drain and set aside. In a mixing bowl, stir together the milk and flour until well combined. Add the butter, eggs, mustard, and salt. Divide the pasta evenly among the cupcake molds. Spoon 1/3 cup cheese into each cup and pour the milk mixture evenly over the top. Bake 20 to 30 minutes until set and browned on top. Cool a few minutes before removing from the pans.

As newborn babes, desire the pure milk of the word, that you may grow thereby, if indeed you have tasted that the Lord is gracious.
[1 Peter 2:2–3]

For if you have been regenerated to Christ,
He who has regenerated us nourishes us with His own milk, the Word.
[Clement of Alexandria, c.150–c.215]

"Was the milk nice?" asked Grandfather. "I never drank any so good before," answered Heidi.
"Then you must have some more."
[*Heidi*, Johanna Spyri, 1827–1901]

TICKET OFFICE

NEXT SHOW

STRAWBERRY FRUIT DIP

A great way to encourage children to eat their fruit!

Makes 3 cups

1/2 pint vanilla yogurt
1 (8-ounce) container whipped topping
1 cup crushed strawberries
2 cups assorted fresh fruit

In a medium bowl combine the yogurt and whipped topping. Stir in the crushed strawberries. Chill until ready to serve. Surround with assorted fresh fruit.

If for an instant God forgot that I am just a puppet, and he gave me one more piece of life, I would take advantage of that time the best I could. I would dress simpler and wallow in the sunlight, exposing my body and my soul . . . [I would tell you] keep always close to you your dear ones and tell them how much you need them and love them. Take care of them. Take time to say, "I am sorry," "forgive me," "please," "thank you," and all the nice and lovely words you know.
[Gabriel Garcia Márquez, 1982 Nobel Prize Laureate in Literature, 1927–]

HONEY LEMON CHICKEN WING DRUMETTES

These also make great football party snacks.
Add some red pepper to spice them up.

Makes 12 wings

1/2 cup all-purpose flour
1 teaspoon Lawry's seasoned salt
12 chicken wing drumettes (1 1/2 to 2 pounds)
1/4 cup honey
1/4 cup lemon juice
1/2 teaspoon soy sauce
1/4 cup butter, melted

Preheat the oven to 350 degrees. Combine the flour and seasoned salt in a paper bag. Add the chicken pieces and shake to coat.

In a small pan over low heat, combine the honey, lemon juice, and soy sauce and heat through.

Place a piece of heavy-duty aluminum foil in the bottom of a 9 x 13-inch baking dish. Pour the butter evenly in the dish. Place the chicken in the dish and turn to coat evenly with the butter. Bake for 15 minutes. Remove from the oven, turn the legs, and baste with the honey mixture. Return to the oven and repeat this step 2 more times until the legs are browned and crusty. Cook time will vary with the size of the drumettes.

Serve with plenty of napkins!

For Our Little Guests

It was on train dinning cars in the 1930s that menus designed especially for children first appeared. They were often shaped like locomotives and were frequently placed in addressed envelopes. Peppermint treats were included for "polite travelers." During this same time everyone's favorite book, *The Little Engine That Could,* was published. It is commonly assumed that the story of the bright blue engine loaded with fruits and vegetables for all the good little boys and girls on the other side of the mountain was written by Watty Piper. It actually first appeared as a sermon on expansive optimism, written by
Rev. Charles S. Wing, in 1906.

CHILDREN'S MENU

CHICKEN DRUMETTES
MACARONI AND CHEESE
MEAT BALLS
CHEESE AND CORN SOUP

FRUIT DIP
TEA CAKES
BERRY TART
APPLE PIE

COUNTRY APPLE PIE

So easy and fun for the children to help prepare.

Makes 1 (9-inch) pie

Pie
4 large, tart apples
1 (9-inch) deep-dish pie shell, unbaked
1/2 cup granulated sugar
1 teaspoon cinnamon

Topping
1/2 cup granulated sugar
3/4 cup all-purpose flour
1/3 cup butter
vanilla caramel swirl ice cream, optional

Preheat the oven to 450 degrees.

To make the pie: Peel, core, and thinly slice the apples. Place the apples in the unbaked pie shell and sprinkle with the sugar and cinnamon.

To make the topping: In a small bowl use a pastry blender or two knives to cut the sugar, flour, and butter together until crumbly. Sprinkle evenly over the apples. Bake for 10 minutes, then reduce the heat to 350 degrees and bake for 40 more minutes. Serve warm with vanilla caramel swirl ice cream.

You are worried about seeing him spend his early years
in doing nothing. What! Is it nothing to be happy? Nothing to skip, play, and run around all day long?
Never in his life will he be so busy again.
[Jean Jacques Rousseau, 1712–1778]

Joy finds its counterpart in the sunshine and the flowers and the birds and the little children,
and enters easily into all the movements of life.
[Hugh Black, 1868–1953]

Remember now your Creator
in the days of your youth.
[Ecclesiastes 12:1]

BARBEQUE MEATBALLS

Serves 3 to 4

Meatballs

1 pound ground chuck

1/2 cup finely minced mild onion

1 large egg, beaten

1/4 cup milk

1/4 cup saltine crackers, crushed

1 teaspoon salt

1/4 teaspoon black pepper, optional

2 tablespoons vegetable oil

Sauce

2 (8-ounce) cans plain tomato sauce

1/4 cup brown sugar

1 teaspoon Lawry's seasoned salt

2 tablespoons red balsamic vinegar

To make the meatballs: In a large bowl combine the ground chuck, onion, egg, milk, crackers, salt, and pepper. Shape the mixture into 16 to 20 meatballs. Heat the oil in a medium skillet and brown the meatballs on all sides. Remove from the pan and pour off the oil.

To make the sauce: In a small bowl combine the tomato sauce, brown sugar, seasoned salt, and vinegar. Pour the sauce into the skillet and add the meatballs back to the pan. Cook, uncovered, over low heat until the meat is thoroughly done and the sauce has thickened.

Our greatest natural resource is the minds of our children.
[Walter Elias Disney, 1901–1966]

All your children shall be taught by the LORD,
And great shall be the peace of your children.
[Isaiah 54:13]

And these words which I command you shall be in your heart. You shall teach them diligently to your
children, and shall talk of them when you sit in your house, when you walk by the way,
when you lie down, and when you rise up.
[Deuteronomy 6:6–7]

FRESH BERRY PIZZA

Children love to decorate the top of this pie!

Serves 8 to 10

1 (18-ounce) roll refrigerated sugar cookie dough
1 (8-ounce) package cream cheese, softened
1 (7-ounce) jar marshmallow cream
4 cups assorted berries, such as strawberries,
  raspberries, blackberries, and blueberries

Preheat the oven to 350 degrees.

With a rolling pin, roll the dough into a 12-inch round and pat the dough into a 12-inch pizza pan. Cook for 18 to 22 minutes. Let cool.

In a small bowl combine the cream cheese and marshmallow cream until blended. Spread over the cookie crust. Decorate the top with assorted berries. Chill until ready to serve.

You, therefore, who teach one another, do you not teach yourself?
[Romans 2:21]

But you must continue in the things which you have learned and been assured of, knowing from whom you have learned them, and that from childhood you have known the Holy Scriptures, which are able to make you wise for salvation through faith which is in Jesus Christ.
[2 Timothy 3:14–15]

"In His name to all the nations"
[Luke 24:47]

INTERNATIONAL CUISINE

I live my life in widening rings
Which spread over earth and sky.
I may not ever complete the last one,
But that is what I will try.
I circle around God, the primordial tower,
And I circle ten thousand years long;
And I still don't know if I'm a falcon, a storm,
Or an unfinished song.
[Rainer Maria Rilke, 1875–1926]

Sing to the LORD a new song, and His praise from the ends of the earth.
[Isaiah 42:10]

In this chapter we have composed for you a new song, a litany of spiritual hospitality. The response we hope to elicit is one in which, with increased cultural sensitivity, in ever widening rings, we might find new ways to enjoy intimate fellowship with those significantly different from ourselves. Please view the last image of the section (page 154) as an artistic rendering of this one-to-one dynamic.

In Genesis 12, we learn that through Abraham the Lord made clear His intention to bless all the communities of the earth. The following was written poignantly and befittingly at a kitchen table: "The end is reconciliation; the end is redemption; the end is the creation of the beloved community" [Dr. Martin Luther King, Jr., 1929–1968].

As we have done throughout this entire book, we continue to follow the advice of an early Church father, Basil of Caesarea, St. Basil the Great [330–379], who suggested that "we must be familiar with poets, historians, orators, in fact everyone who can help our souls to salvation." We deliberately focus on physical nourishment because, as President Woodrow Wilson [1856–1924] once put it, "No one can worship God or love his neighbor on an empty stomach. In the Lord's Prayer, the first petition is for daily bread!" These voices serve as accompaniment to our colorful collage of fusion at its finest.

It takes great courage to open the doors of our homes to outsiders. In making the decision to share our private lives in this manner, we turn for inspiration to the thousands of international missionaries who for centuries have dedicated themselves to this endeavor. We offer the following chapter as a quiet tribute to their faithfulness. And may you, like them, in the extending of radical hospitality, feel the unexpected embrace of God's own gracious spirit.

And how is it that we hear, each in our own language in which we were born?
. . . Those dwelling in Mesopotamia . . . Asia . . . Egypt . . . Libya . . . visitors from Rome . . . Jews . . .
Cretans and Arabs—we hear them speaking in our own tongues the wonderful works of God . . .
saying to one another,
"Whatever could this mean?"
[Acts 2:8–12]

INTERNATIONAL CUISINE

Gazpacho

Candied Yams

Pollo San Miguel

Beef and Broccoli Stir-Fry

Cheddar Pecan Scones

*Veal, Prosciutto, and Portobello Fettuccini
with Sun-Dried Tomato Sauce*

Creamy Feta Dressing

Pear Tarts

Then to Him was
given dominion
and glory and a kingdom,
That all peoples, nations, and
languages should serve Him.
His dominion is an
everlasting dominion,
Which shall not pass away,
And His kingdom the one
Which shall not be destroyed.
[Daniel 7:14]

GAZPACHO

For a special treat, top each bowl of soup with a grilled, butterflied shrimp.

Serves 8

2 cloves garlic, minced
1 small red onion, diced
1 large English cucumber, diced
1 carrot, diced
2 stalks celery, diced
1 yellow bell pepper, diced
1 red bell pepper, diced
1 (36-ounce) container V-8 juice
1/4 cup extra virgin olive oil
2 tablespoons red wine vinegar
1/4 cup lemon juice
1 teaspoon sugar
Tabasco to taste
salt and pepper to taste

In a large bowl combine the garlic, onion, cucumber, carrot, celery, and peppers. Stir in the V-8 juice, olive oil, vinegar, lemon juice, sugar, Tabasco, salt, and pepper. Chill for several hours or overnight, if possible.

Note: If a finer texture is desired, the soup may be pureed in batches in a food processor.

There is not one blade of grass, there is no color in
this world that is not intended to make us rejoice.
[John Calvin, 1509–1564]

God is liberal of color; so should man be.
[Herman Melville, 1819–1891]

True Godliness does not turn men out of the world,
but enables them to live better in it and excites their endeavors to mend it.
{William Penn, 1644–1718}

CANDIED YAMS

Serves 3 to 4

2 large yams or sweet potatoes (1/2 pound each)
1/4 cup butter
1/2 cup light brown sugar
1/2 teaspoon ground cinnamon

Preheat the oven to 400 degrees.

In a medium pot cover the unpeeled whole potatoes with water and simmer over low heat until almost done, about 40 minutes. Drain and let cool a few minutes. Peel and slice into 1-inch rounds.

In a small bowl combine the butter, brown sugar, and cinnamon.

In a 1-quart round casserole dish, arrange the first potato in an overlapping circle. Dot with the brown sugar mixture. Repeat the layer with the second potato and cover with the remaining brown sugar mixture.

Bake uncovered 20 to 30 minutes, until bubbly, basting a few times with the remaining brown sugar mixture.

You know sometimes I sit
and wonder just how this world would be
If we had all the people laughing and everybody living in harmony.

It's time you know for everyone to come together
I know it's hard but this dream must come to light.

Because life should be one big celebration
I'm talking to you now
Only we can make things right.
[Lionel Richie, 1949–]

After these things I looked,
and behold, a great multitude which no one could number,
of all nations, tribes, peoples, and tongues,
standing before the throne and before the Lamb,
clothed with white robes, with palm branches in their hands.
[Revelation 7:9]

POLLO SAN MIGUEL

Serves 4 to 6

2 tablespoons butter
2 tablespoons vegetable oil
6 boneless, skinless chicken breasts (1/2 pound each)
2 (14-ounce) cans refried beans
1 (8-ounce) jar roasted chipotle salsa
Tabasco sauce, optional
2 cups grated Monterey Jack cheese

Preheat oven to 350 degrees.

Heat the butter and oil in a large skillet over medium-high heat and brown the chicken breasts on both sides. Remove from the heat and place the breasts in a large flat baking dish.

Combine the beans and salsa and pour evenly over each breast. Sprinkle with Tabasco sauce, if desired. Cover the dish and bake 30 to 40 minutes, until the chicken is tender. Uncover and sprinkle with the grated cheese. Bake a few more minutes uncovered until the cheese is melted and bubbly.

And where do you come from?
What is your country?
And of what people are you?
[Jonah 1:8]

For by one Spirit we were baptized into one body . . .
and have all been made to drink into one Spirit.
[1 Corinthians 12:13]

Our ability to reach unity in diversity will be the beauty and test of our civilization.
[Mohandas Karamchand Gandhi, 1869–1948]

BEEF AND BROCCOLI STIR-FRY

Serves 4

2 teaspoons sesame oil
2 large garlic cloves, minced
1/2 teaspoon crushed red pepper
1 pound lean boneless sirloin steak about 3/4-inch-thick,
 cut across the grain into 2 x 1/4-inch strips
3 tablespoons vegetable oil, divided
1 large sweet onion, halved and sliced
1 cup beef broth, divided
4 ounces fresh shiitake mushrooms, stems removed and thinly sliced
3/4 pound broccoli florets
1 large red bell pepper, cut into 2 x 1/4-inch strips
2 tablespoons soy sauce, divided
1 1/2 teaspoons cornstarch
6 cups cooked long-grain white rice

In a medium bowl combine the sesame oil, garlic, and red pepper. Add the meat and marinate 20 minutes. Remove the meat from the marinade. Heat a wok or large heavy skillet until hot but not smoking. Add 2 tablespoons vegetable oil to the pan. Stir-fry the meat in three batches, browning quickly on both sides. Remove from the pan.

Wipe out the pan and add 1 tablespoon oil. Add the onion and stir-fry for 1 minute until it begins to brown. Stir in 1/2 cup of the beef broth and add the mushrooms, broccoli, and red pepper to the pan. Sprinkle with 1 tablespoon soy sauce. Cook, stirring frequently, until the broccoli is tender.

In a small bowl mix the cornstarch with 1/2 cup beef broth and add to the pan. Cook until slightly thickened. Taste for seasoning and add more soy sauce and red pepper, if needed. Serve with white rice.

Differences are not intended to separate, to alienate.
We are different precisely in order to recognize our need for one another.
[Desmond Tutu, 1931–]

We are aliens and pilgrims before You, as were all our fathers.
[1 Chronicles 29:15]

CHEDDAR PECAN SCONES

A delicious treat for breakfast served with jam or butter.

Serves 12

2 1/2 cups self-rising flour
1 teaspoon baking powder
1/2 teaspoon dry mustard
pinch cayenne pepper
1/4 cup unsalted butter
1 cup grated sharp cheddar cheese
1 cup buttermilk, plus additional for brushing the top of scones
1/2 cup chopped pecans

Preheat the oven to 400 degrees.

In a large bowl whisk together the flour, baking powder, dry mustard, and cayenne pepper. Blend in the butter with a pastry blender until the mixture resembles coarse meal. Stir in the cheese, buttermilk, and pecans to make a soft dough.

Turn out the dough on a lightly floured surface. Gently knead 3 or 4 times. Divide the dough in 3 parts and pat each part into a 6-inch circle. Cut each circle into 6 triangles. Transfer to a buttered cookie sheet and brush the tops with buttermilk. Bake 16 to 18 minutes, until golden brown. Remove the scones to a cooling rack. Serve warm.

Note: These may be cut out with a 3-inch cookie cutter if you prefer a smaller scone.

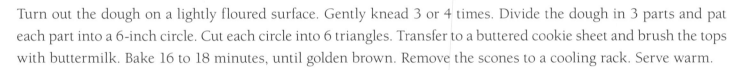
"For My name shall be great among
the nations," says the LORD of hosts.
[Malachi 1:11]

So shall one Nation's song ascend
To Thee our Ruler, Father, Friend,
While heaven's wide arch resounds again
With peace on earth, good will to men.
{Oliver Wendell Holmes, 1809–1894}

VEAL, PROSCIUTTO, AND PORTOBELLO FETTUCCINI WITH SUN-DRIED TOMATO SAUCE

Serves 4 to 6

4 to 6 tablespoons corn oil, divided

1 pound very thinly sliced Prosciutto di Parma, cut in small pieces

1 1/2 pounds veal scallops, cut into bite-size pieces

1 cup all-purpose flour, divided

12 ounces portobello mushrooms, cut into 1-inch pieces

1 large mild onion, chopped

1/2 cup veal or beef stock

1/4 cup Marsala wine, optional

1 teaspoon dried thyme

1 cup milk or half-and-half

1/4 cup sun-dried tomato spread (or slivered sun-dried tomato pieces)

1 pound dry fettuccini, cooked

2 ounces Parmigiano-Reggiano cheese, to grate

Add 2 tablespoons oil to a large skillet over medium heat. Sauté the Prosciutto until crisp. Remove from the pan and drain on paper towels.

Sprinkle the veal with about 1/2 cup of flour and add to the skillet. Sauté the meat in four batches, adding more oil if needed. Remove from the pan and set aside. Wipe out the pan and add 2 more tablespoons oil. Place the mushrooms and onion in the pan and cover the pan. Sweat the vegetables until the onions are translucent and the mushrooms have released their juice. Add the Prosciutto, veal, stock, wine, and thyme to the pan. Cover and cook 20 minutes until the meat is very tender.

In a small bowl whisk 3 tablespoons flour into the milk until smooth. Add the sun-dried tomatoes to the milk mixture and pour into the skillet. Cook uncovered until the sauce is creamy. Place the pasta on a serving platter and pour the sauce over top. Sprinkle with freshly grated Parmigiano-Reggiano cheese.

It's not right to prefer this food or that food . . .

Thus spake Tenzin Gyatso, the Dalai Lama, who appeared as a judge on a popular Australian cooking show in the summer of 2011. He went on to point out that all the cooks had "done their best." This was the perfect response for someone who at another time expressed the following beautiful hope.

I pray for a more caring and understanding human family ...
"We" and "they" no longer exist. The planet is just us.

CREAMY FETA DRESSING

Makes 2 1/2 cups

2 cloves garlic
1/4 cup red wine vinegar
1 1/2 teaspoons Worcestershire sauce
1/2 teaspoon each dried oregano, thyme, and basil
   (or 1 1/2 teaspoons if fresh)
1 1/2 cups crumbled Feta cheese, divided
1 cup good quality mayonnaise (Hellman's preferred)
2 tablespoons extra virgin olive oil

In a blender pulse the garlic with the vinegar. Add the Worcestershire, herbs, 1/2 cup Feta cheese, and the mayonnaise. Add the olive oil and pulse to a creamy consistency. Stir in the remaining cup of Feta cheese. Serve with fresh or grilled vegetables.

Turn, turn, my wheel! The human race,
Of every tongue, of every place,
Caucasian, Coptic, or Malay
All that inhabit this great earth,
Whatever be their rank or worth,
Are kindred and allied by birth
And made of the same clay.
[Henry Wadsworth Longfellow, 1807–1882]

The road to holiness necessarily passes through the world of action.
[Dag Hjalmar Agne Carl Hammarskjold, 1905–1961]

Pear Tarts

So easy and elegant!

Makes 4 6-inch tarts

1 (1 pound) package puff pastry sheets (2 sheets)
4 or 5 Bosc pears (1/2 pound each)
1 tablespoon butter
2 tablespoons white sparkling sugar
vanilla ice cream, optional

Preheat the oven to 425 degrees.

Roll out the pastry to a 1/4-inch thickness and cut two 6- to 7-inch circles from each sheet using a saucer as a guide. Place on a baking sheet lined with parchment paper.

Core the pears and cut into thin crescents. Arrange the pears on the pastry pinwheel style. Dot with butter and sprinkle with the sugar. Bake for 20 minutes until puffed and golden. Serve warm with a scoop of vanilla ice cream.

Note: Leftover scraps can be cut into shapes, sprinkled with sugar, and cooked as treats for the children.

Whether the food is peasant or gourmet,
Long prepared or merely made in haste,
Served on silver or on wooden tray,
Love makes the meal to everybody's taste.
[Jatakas 346, fourth century BC]

So they sat down, and the two of them ate and drank together.
[Judges 19:6]

Please spend the night.
[Judges 19:9]

Blessed by Guests Who Stay Awhile

Make yourself a guest chamber in your own house. Set up a bed there, set up a table there and a candle stick.
Say, "This is Christ's space." Even if it is a basement and tiny, He won't refuse it. Knowing this, let us receive the saints
that the house may shine, that the bed chamber may become a haven.
[John Chrysostom, 347–407]

This early archbishop of Constantinople was no stranger to biblical precedent. He knew well the story of the widow who appealed to her husband to build such a facility for the prophet Elisha:

Look now, I know that this is a holy man of God, who passes by us regularly. Please, let us make a small upper room
on the wall; and let us put a bed for him there, and a table and a chair and a lampstand; so it will be, whenever he
comes to us, he can turn in there.
[2 Kings 4:9–12]

Because Greek was native to Chrysostom, he was also well aware that the words *inn* and *guest room* were often interchangeable. It saddened him to think that the inn that had no room for the birth of our Lord and the room where He partook of His last meal were both commercial establishments. These sentiments became somewhat of a battle cry for hospitality, and throughout the medieval period people often built guest houses in case the Holy Family reappeared. If you or anyone you know is debating the value of "adding on" to a home, perhaps these thoughts might give the argument a new perspective!

Having guests who stay awhile involves hard work on the part of everyone involved. The travail of preparing to receive is often mirrored by the stress of those who travel. The words are in the same family and alert us to the fact that at the moment of arrival everyone may not be at their best. For this reason we have assembled a number of selections that can be prepared in advance, allowing you to actually enjoy the many blessings that accompany the arrival of each and every guest.

Blest be the spot, where cheerful guests retire
To pause from toil, and trim their evening fire;
Blest be that abode, where want and pain repair,
And every stranger finds a ready chair;
Blest be those feasts with simple plenty crowned,
Where all the ruddy family round . . .
Press the bashful stranger to his food,
And learn the luxury of doing good.
[Oliver Goldsmith, 1730–1774]

As our time together comes to a close, the collaborators of *Share the Bounty* heartily thank you for joining us, as together we have sought ways to practice hospitality as a manifestation of Christian faith. Upon retiring, we invite you to copy any of the *bons mots*, the happy thoughts, that we have included in these pages. Why not place one on the pillow of your guest's bed as a charming way of saying to your fine company, as we now say to you, "*Bon Soir!*"

BLESSED BY GUESTS WHO STAY AWHILE

Sun-Dried Tomato Spread

Mushroom Goat Cheese Puffs

Basil Chicken Salad

Gene's Chili

Applesauce Cranberry Muffins

Blueberry Peach Coffee Cake

Ham Croissant Casserole

Cajun Shrimp and Grits Casserole

Fig Turnovers

Heaven is My throne,
And earth is My footstool.
What house will you build for Me?
says the LORD,
Or what is the place of My rest?
Has My hand not made all these things?
[Acts 7:49–50]

When you lie down, you will not be afraid;
Yes, you will lie down
and your sleep will be sweet.
[Proverbs 3:24]

SUN-DRIED TOMATO SPREAD

Serves 6 to 8

1/4 cup sun-dried tomatoes in oil, chopped

11 ounces soft goat cheese

1/2 cup unsalted butter

1 tablespoon chopped fresh basil

Pour 2 tablespoons of oil from the tomatoes and set aside. Discard the remaining oil. In a food processor, pulse the oil, goat cheese, and butter until mixed. Add the tomatoes and basil and pulse until well blended. Spoon the mixture into a small serving bowl and chill for several hours. Serve at room temperature with unseasoned crackers.

Happy is the house that shelters a friend.
[Ralph Waldo Emerson, 1803–1882]

And now good-morrow to our waking souls,
Which watch not one another out of fear;
For love all love of other sights controls,
And makes one little room an everywhere.
[John Donne, 1572–1631]

We can easily forgive a child who is afraid of the dark;
The real tragedy of life is when men are afraid of the light.
[Plato, 427–347 BC]

Mushroom Goat Cheese Puffs

Makes 36

1 tablespoon butter

1 tablespoon minced shallot

4 ounces mushrooms, finely chopped

4 ounces goat cheese with herbs at room temperature

1 teaspoon lemon juice

1 sheet frozen puff pastry (half of a 17.3-ounce package),
   defrosted

1 egg yolk, beaten with 1 teaspoon water for egg wash

Preheat the oven to 400 degrees.

Melt the butter in a small sauté pan over medium heat. Add
the shallot and mushrooms and cook until soft. Let cool.

In a medium bowl stir the goat cheese with the lemon juice and mix with the cooled mushrooms.

Thinly roll out the puff pastry and cut into 3 strips at the fold lines. Spread 1/3 of the mushroom mixture down
one strip. Moisten one long side with water and roll up the strip like a jelly roll. Press to seal the edge. Repeat with
the remaining strips. Cut each strip into 12 pieces and place seam side down on a parchment-lined baking sheet.
Brush the tops lightly with the egg wash. Bake until puffed and golden brown, about 10 minutes.

Note: These may be frozen before baking and cooked frozen a few extra minutes.

Please be content to stay all night,
and let your heart be merry.
[Judges 19:6]

Why did they not stay that we might have had their company?
Are we not all on the same pilgrimage?
[John Bunyan, 1628–1688]

BASIL CHICKEN SALAD

This refreshing salad is nice to have on hand for guests as a snack or late-night sandwich.

Makes 1 quart

3 cups chopped cooked chicken (rotisserie is fine)
1/2 cup mayonnaise
1/2 cup sour cream
1/2 cup loosely packed fresh basil, chopped
3 green onions, minced
1 cup finely chopped celery
salt and pepper to taste

In a medium bowl combine the chicken, mayonnaise, sour cream, basil, onions, and celery. Add salt and pepper to taste. Chill several hours or overnight for flavors to blend.

"Now whatever city or town you enter,
inquire who in it is worthy, and stay there till you go out."
[Matthew 10:11]

Stay is a charming word in a friend's vocabulary.
[Louisa May Alcott, 1832–1888]

Look, the day is now drawing toward evening; please spend the night.
[Judges 19:9]

GENE'S CHILI

The whole cloves add an interesting, spicy flavor.

Serves 6

2 pounds ground chuck
1 large sweet onion, very finely diced
2 tablespoons vegetable oil
2 (14.5-ounce) cans pureed tomatoes
2 (14-ounce) can Mexican-style chili beans
2 teaspoons sea salt
1/4 teaspoon paprika
1/4 teaspoon cayenne pepper (or to taste)
4 tablespoons chili powder
3 whole bay leaves
6 whole cloves
1 small piece of cheesecloth
1 cup shredded cheddar cheese, optional

In a heavy saucepan over medium-high heat, brown the meat and onions in the oil. Add the tomatoes, beans, salt, paprika, cayenne pepper, and chili powder. Tie the bay leaves and cloves in a small piece of cheesecloth and place in the pan. Simmer covered, for 1 hour, stirring frequently. Remove the spice bag. Serve topped with shredded cheddar cheese, if desired.

But he insisted strongly,
so they turned in to him and entered his house.
Then he made them a feast.
[Genesis 19:3]

So it was, as often as he passed by, he would turn in there to eat some food.
[2 Kings 4:8]

I will both lie down in peace, and sleep;
For You alone, O Lord, make me dwell in safety.
[Psalm 4:8]

For every kind of beast and bird...
is tamed and has been tamed by mankind.
But no man can tame the tongue.
[James 3:7–8]

APPLESAUCE CRANBERRY MUFFINS

Makes 12 large muffins

1 1/4 cups granulated sugar
1/2 cup butter, softened
2 large eggs
1 3/4 cups applesauce
3/4 cup milk
1 cup dried cranberries
2 1/2 cups all-purpose flour
3/4 teaspoon baking soda
1/4 teaspoon baking powder
1/2 teaspoon salt
1 teaspoon pumpkin pie spice
1/2 cup chopped pecans
1/4 cup light brown sugar

Preheat the oven to 375 degrees and grease 12 muffin tins.

In a large bowl cream the sugar and butter together. Beat in the eggs. Add in the applesauce, milk, and cranberries and stir with a spatula until combined.

In a medium bowl sift together the flour, baking soda, baking powder, salt, and pumpkin pie spice. Add the dry ingredients to the wet ingredients and gently mix to combine. The batter will still be lumpy. Don't over mix. Add the pecans.

Pour the batter into the muffin tins. Sprinkle one teaspoon of light brown sugar on top of each cup. Bake for 20 minutes or until a cake tester comes out clean.

"I do not want to send them away hungry,
lest they faint on the way."
[Matthew 15:32]

Blessed be the LORD, who has given rest to His people Israel,
according to all that He promised.
[1 Kings 8:56]

BLUEBERRY PEACH COFFEE CAKE

Delicious toasted with butter.

Serves 8 to 10

2 cups plus 2 tablespoons all-purpose flour

2 teaspoons baking powder

1/2 teaspoon salt

1/4 cup unsalted butter, softened

3/4 cup granulated sugar

1 large egg

1/2 cup milk

2 cups blueberries

2 cups chopped peaches

1/4 cup unsalted butter, softened

1/2 cup granulated sugar

1/3 cup light brown sugar

1 teaspoon ground cinnamon

Preheat the oven to 350 degrees.

In a medium bowl sift together 2 cups flour, baking powder, and salt. Set aside. In a large bowl cream the butter and sugar until fluffy. Beat in the egg. Add the flour mixture to the butter mixture in 3 parts, alternating with the milk. The mixture will be thick. Toss the blueberries and peaches with the remaining flour and pour into the batter, mixing gently. Pour the batter into a greased 9-inch springform pan.

For the topping, in a small bowl combine the butter, sugars, and cinnamon with a fork until crumbly. Sprinkle over the batter in the pan. Bake for 50 to 60 minutes until a cake tester inserted in the center of the cake comes out clean. Let cool in the pan a few minutes before removing.

But, meanwhile, also prepare a guest room for me,
for I trust that through your prayers I shall be granted to you.
[Philemon v. 22]

Mighty proud am I that I am able to have a spare bed for my friends.
[Samuel Pepys, 1633–1703]

Ham Croissant Casserole

Serves 8

4 large day-old croissants, split and toasted
1/2 pound chopped ham
6 ounces shredded sharp cheddar cheese
1/3 cup finely shredded Parmesan cheese
8 large eggs
3 cups milk
1 1/2 tablespoons Dijon mustard
1 teaspoon salt
pepper to taste
Tabasco sauce, optional

Butter a 2-quart baking dish. Alternately arrange, cut side down, croissant halves and chopped ham. Sprinkle with the cheeses. Set aside.

Whisk together the eggs, milk, mustard, salt, pepper, and Tabasco sauce. Pour over the casserole, cover with plastic wrap, and refrigerate overnight.

Preheat the oven to 350 degrees. Bake uncovered about 1 hour and 30 minutes. Tent it loosely with foil if it starts to brown too quickly. Let stand 15 minutes before serving.

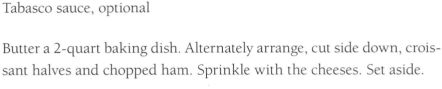

Dawn upon this soul of mine.
Word of God and inward light
Wake my spirit, clear my sight.
[Samuel Longfellow, 1819–1892]

Cajun Shrimp and Grits Casserole

Serves 6 to 8

1/3 pound Andouille sausage, diced

2 cups water

2 cups milk

2 tablespoons butter

1/2 teaspoon salt

1 cup stone ground grits

2 cups grated Monterey Jack cheese, divided

1 cup sour cream

2 eggs, beaten

1/3 cup chopped green onion

1/4 cup minced parsley

2 cups peeled and cooked shrimp

salt and pepper to taste

Preheat the oven to 350 degrees.

In a small skillet cook the sausage until lightly brown. Set aside.

Pour the water and milk into a heavy saucepan and bring to a boil over medium heat. Add the butter, salt, and grits and stir over medium heat until the mixture comes to a boil again. Reduce the heat to low, cover, and simmer for 20 minutes, stirring frequently. Add a little extra water if the mixture thickens too quickly.

Fold in the sausage, 1 cup cheese, sour cream, eggs, green onion, parsley, and shrimp. Taste for seasonings. Place the mixture in a greased casserole and top with the remaining cheese. Bake for 30 minutes until set in the center.

Note: For a spicier casserole use Pepper Jack cheese.

Then as he lay and slept . . .
an angel touched him, and said to him,
"Arise and eat."
[1 Kings 19:5]

Jesus said to them, "Come and eat breakfast."
[John 21:12]

FIG TURNOVERS

These little pies freeze well and any kind of preserves may be used for filling.

Serves 24

2 (9-inch) refrigerated roll-out piecrusts
jar of fig preserves
1 egg white, lightly beaten
sparkling sugar sprinkles

Preheat oven to 375 degrees.

On a floured surface roll the dough out thinly. Using a 3-inch cookie cutter, stamp out 12 circles from each piecrust. You may have to piece together the last few circles.

Place 3/4 teaspoon of preserves in the middle of each circle. Brush the edges with a little water and fold the circles into a half-moon shape. Crimp the edges with a fork to seal. Brush the tops with a little egg wash and sprinkle with the sugar. Bake 15 minutes until golden brown.

My bed is waiting cool and fresh
with linen smooth and fair,
And I must be off to sleepsin, by and not forget my prayer.

I know that, till to–morrow I shall see the sun arise,
No ugly dream shall fright my mind, no ugly sight my eyes.

But slumber hold me tightly till I waken in the dawn,
And hear the thrushes singing in the lilacs round the lawn.
[Robert Louis Stevenson, 1850–1894]

The Singing in God's Acre

Out yonder in the moonlight, wherein God's acre lies,
Go angels walking to and fro, singing their lullabies.
Their radiant wings are folded, and their eyes are bended low,
As they sing among the beds whereon the flowers delight to grow,

The flowers within God's acre see that fair and wondrous sight,
And hear the angels singing to the sleepers through the night;
And lo! throughout the hours of day those gentle flowers prolong
The music of the angels in that tender slumber song.

Sleep, oh sleep!
The Shepherd loveth His sheep.
He that guardeth His flock the best
Hath folded them to His loving breast;
So sleep ye now and take your rest,
Sleep, oh, sleep!
[Eugene Field, 1850–1895]

Say "Amen" at your giving of thanks

[1 Corinthians 14:16]

PRAYERS OF GRATITUDE

Grant to us the wonderous blessings in rich

abundance which this day was designed to impart.

May it be wholly consecrated to You. May a halo
of heavenly mindedness sparkle around us.

We are invited to precious delights. The banqueting
house of Thy word is widely open.

Eat, O friends; drink, yea drink abundantly, beloved.
Eat ye that which is good.

May we sit down under our Lord's shadow,
and may we find His fruit sweet to our taste.
[*Family Prayers*, Henry Law, 1797–1884]

The eyes of all look expectantly to
You, and You give them their food in due season.
You open Your hand
And satisfy the desire of every living thing.
[Psalm 145:15–16]

☙

Two things I request of You . . .
Give me neither poverty nor riches—
Feed me with the food allotted to me;
Lest I be full and deny You, . . .
Or lest I be poor and steal.
[Proverbs 30:7–9]

☙

If you offer only one prayer to God,
make it one of thanksgiving.
[Meister Eckhart, 1260–1327]

Oh, that men would give thanks to the
LORD for His goodness
And for His wonderful works to the
children of men!
For He satisfies the longing soul,
And fills the hungry soul with goodness.
[Psalm 107:8–9]

☙

Dear Mother earth, who day by day,
Unfoldest blessings on our way,
The flowers and fruits that in thee grow,
Let them His glories also show.
[St. Francis of Assisi, 1181–1226]

☙

God, our Provider, we give thanks
for the places we call home. For nations and motherlands, cities and neighborhoods,
places to lay our heads and tables blessed with food, we give You thanks.
[*The African American Heritage Hymnal*, Thanksgiving Litany #99]

Savior, like a Shepherd lead us

Much we need Thy tender care;
In Thy pleasant pastures feed us,
For our use Thy folds prepare.
[Dorothy Ann Thrupp, 1779–1847]

❧

We thank Thee Lord for this our food

But more because of Jesus' love
Let manna to our souls be given
The Bread of Life sent down from Heaven

Be present at our table Lord
Be here and everywhere ador'd
These creatures bless and grant that we
May feast in Paradise with Thee.
[Written by Rev. John Cennick to be inscribed
on a teapot given to John Wesley by Josiah Wedgewood in 1761]

❧

Blessed be You, O Lord,

who has nourished [us] from our youth and who gives food to all flesh. Fill our
hearts with joy and gladness, that having all we need, we may abound in every good
work, in Christ Jesus, through whom glory,
honor and power be to You forever.
[*The Apostolic Constitutions*, VI, fourth century]

Father, propitious be!
On me Thy mercy show!
Bow down Thine ear to me,
On me Thy grace bestow;
For Thine the glory, Thine the grace
While countless ages run their race.
[St. Gregory, 329–390]

God, give us grateful hearts.
For if we do not have the grace to thank Thee for all we have and enjoy,
How can we have the effrontery to seek
Thy further blessings? For Jesus' sake, Amen.
[Peter Marshall, 1902–1949]

Father we thank Thee for the night,
And for the pleasant morning light;
For rest and food and loving care,
And all that makes the day so fair.

Help us to do the things we should,
To be to others kind and good;
In all we do in work or play,
To love Thee better day by day.
[Rebecca Weston, 1835–1895]

I sing the goodness of the Lord,
That filled the earth with food;
He formed the creatures with His word,
And then pronounced them good.

Lord, how Thy wonders are displayed,
Where'er I turn my eye:
If I survey the ground I tread,
Or gaze upon the sky.
[Issac Watts, 1664–1748]

God of the angels,
Creator and ruler of all things, visible and invisible;
We offer heartfelt thanks to You, O God, that You have shown
Such unmerited generosity and kindness to us
and to all manner of all human beings.
All creation praises You for You have created everything and
Through Your will everything exists.
We praise You in all things and for all things.
We bless and glorify You now and forever.
[*The Nunnaminster Codex*, ninth century]

O Lord, our Savior, who hast warned us that
Thou wilt require more of us to whom much is given; grant that we
whose lot is cast in so goodly a heritage may strive together the more
abundantly to extend to others what we so richly enjoy;
so that in their turn others may enter into our labor,
to the fulfillment of Thy holy will;
through Jesus Christ our Lord, Amen.
[St. Augustine, 354–430]

Inscribe my name with favor
Within your Book divine;
And grant my soul to savor
That marriage feast of thine.
Where all the saints assembled
In life abundant dine
There shall I sing forever
Your faithfulness sublime.
[Martin Luther, 1483–1546]

Now to Him who is able to do exceedingly
abundantly above all that we ask or think . . . to Him be glory in the church by
Christ Jesus to all generations, forever and ever.
Amen.
[Ephesians 3:20–21]

Let brotherly love continue

[Hebrews 13:1]

BENEDICTION

May you set your heart on things above

May you set your mind on things above

May you practice truth

May you allow Christ to be your all in all

May you be clothed with

Compassion Kindness Humility Gentleness Patience

Forgive as the Lord forgives you

And over all these virtues may you put on love which

binds them together in perfect communion

May you let the peace of Christ dwell in your heart

May you let the Word of Christ dwell in you

May your home be an expressive home filled with passion

for Christ, for others, for life!

—Steve Wingfield

[Inspired by Galatians 2:20 and Colossians 3:1–7]

Overflowing with thankfulness
[Colossians 2:7 (NIV)]

ACKNOWLEDGMENTS

We heartily thank our community of friends who made this
work not only possible but pleasant in every way.

Therefore, whoever boasts of his own works . . . boasts of what does not exist.
[The Scottish Confession of 1560]

Mr. John Bush Long

Dr. John C. Mitchell (in memorium)

Mr. James T. Wilson, Jr.

Mr. and Mrs. A L. Adams

Judge and Mrs. A. Scott Allen

Mrs. Mary Ann Mell Baggs

Mr. and Mrs. William H. Barrett

Mrs. Thomas W. Blanchard

Mr. Dan Belman

Mr. and Mrs. Brent Boyd

Miss Bentley Boyd

Mrs. Ann Boardman

Mr. and Mrs. Braye C. Boardman

Teri and Mose Bond

Judge and Mrs. Dudley H. Bowen, Jr.

Briar Creek Farms

Camp Boxwoods

Mr. Albert Cheatham

Dr. and Mrs. Joe D. Christian

The Cloister at Sea Island

Mr. and Mrs. Edward E. Crawford

Design Images and Gifts

Mrs. Lawrence Devoe

Distinctly Different Antiques

Mr. and Mrs. Edwin L. Douglass, Jr.

Mrs. A. Z. Everitt

The Faculty and Staff of Erskine Theological Seminary

First Presbyterian Church, Highlands, NC

Mr. and Mrs. Robert Fisher

Georgia State Floral Distributors

Mrs. Rose Garnett

Liz Griffin

Mr. and Mrs. James B. Kay III

Mrs. Alonzo Key

Mr. and Mrs. Cord Kilpatrick

Pinckney and McCord Kilpatrick

Dr. and Mrs. William Rodgers Kitchens

Mrs. Boone A. Knox

Mr. Randy Korando

Mr. and Mrs. Dessie Kuhlke

Mr. and Mrs. William Kuhkle

Mr. and Mrs. John Ryd Bush Long

Miss Sallie Long

Mrs. James Hampton Manning, Jr.

Mr. and Mrs. Mason McKnight

Mr. and Mrs. Benjamin L. Mason

Sara and Jack Mayer

Mr. and Mrs. Finley H. Merry

Mr. Alec Michaelides

Mr. and Mrs. Alan B. Moore, Jr.

Lillie and Tripp Moore

Dr. and Mrs. William Moretz

Mr. and Mrs. Fred Motz

Mr. and Mrs. Sam Nicholson

Mr. and Mrs. James F. Norvell, Jr.

Judge J. Carlisle Overstreet

Dr. and Mrs. Glen Owen

Dr. and Mrs. Edward S. Porubsky

Mrs. Allen Post

Dr. and Mrs. John Reynolds III

Mr. and Mrs. John Robinson

St. Michael's Episcopal Church, Charleston, SC

St. Phillip's Cathedral, Atlanta, GA

Scotlyn's Yard Nursery

Steed's Dairy

Mrs. George W. Thurmond

Mr. and Mrs. James T. Wison III

Salley and Thomas Wilson

Write in a book for yourself all the words

[Jeremiah 30:2]

INDEX